TAKING BIG BUCKS

SOLVING THE WHITETAIL RIDDLE

By Ed Wolff

Published in the United States of America

Taking Big Bucks

SOLVING THE WHITETAIL RIDDLE

By Ed Wolff

Copyright 1987 by Ed Wolff

ISBN 0-912299-25-8 (Hardcover)
ISBN 0-912299-26-6 (Softcover)

Stoneydale Press Publishing Co.
205 Main Street — Drawer B
Stevensville, Montana 59870
Phone: **406-777-2729**

Dedication

This book is dedicated with sincere appreciation to all the men and women, past and present, who were farsighted enough to fight long battles to preserve not only whitetail deer but also the habitat they need to survive. Their personal sacrifice of time and energy has left a legacy for all of us to enjoy.

Gene Wensel says to his knowledge the buck shown here in the timber is the biggest buck ever photographed alive in the wild. It scored 187 B&C points.

Table of Contents

Dedication. . . . . .Page 5
Table of Contents. . . . . .Page 7
Introduction. . . . . .Page 9
History of Whitetail Hunting. . . . . .Page 17
Characteristics and Habitat. . . . . .Page 23
Management and Population Dynamics. . . . . .Page 47
The Rut and Hunting Theory. . . . . .Page 65
Hunting the Rocky Mountain Whitetail. . . . . .Page 75
The Whitetail Mystique. . . . . .Page 103
Gene Wensel. . . . . .Page 115
Barry Wensel. . . . . .Page 129
Tom Dellwo. . . . . .Page 141
Dick Idol. . . . . .Page 151
Conclusion. . . . . .Page 169

COVER PHOTO

Author Ed Wolff took the cover photograph of these two fine, trophy whitetail bucks within an hour of his Montana home. They exemplify both the beauty and mystique of the trophy whitetail deer.

The best two bucks ever taken in Montana. On the left is the number one which is also ranked Number 6 in the world, scoring 199 3/8 B&C points. Both bucks were taken in the rough mountains of the Seeley-Swan valley.

Introduction

First, I would like to tell you what this book isn't. Then you can decide whether to read on or forget it.

It is not about how to field dress a deer, the best rifle or bow with which to take deer, where to shoot a deer for an instant kill, or another tome about ho-hum deer hunting stories. These subjects along, with dozens of others, have been hashed and rehashed by numerous writers to the point of turning one's stomach. It is not purely and simply another boring "how to book," of which there are dozens in circulation. I'm not going to sit here and tell you I'm "the" expert whitetail hunter. I've killed my share, but I'm still learning from the likes of Gene Wensel, Barry Wensel, and Dick Idol. These gentlemen are a few of the true experts in the art of slaying big bucks on a regular basis. They work at their craft very hard, 12 months a year, year in and year out. Therein lies their individual secrets — sincere dedication, hard work, and paying attention to detail.

My purpose for writing this book is threefold.

First, I've been numbed by the voluminous amounts of information currently being written and spoken describing the various facets of whitetail hunting. This book will sift through the multitude of whitetail theories proposed by the pseudo-experts and the true experts alike. Much new information has appeared in print during the past two to three years — the meaning of scrapes and rubs and whitetail behavior in general, to name a few. This information needs to be examined and critiqued.

Second, I want to introduce you the the tremendous whitetail hunting in the Northern Rockies. (The Northern Rockies as presented in this text is an area encompassed roughly by a line through Billings, Montana, running perpendicular through Montana from the Canadian border south to the northern border of Wyoming. Then go west in a line running through Salmon, Idaho, to the Washington state line. Then go north to the Canadian border and hence west to intersect the north-south line through Billings.) The mountainous areas west of the Continental Divide in Montana and Idaho are rapidly becoming premier whitetail areas producing exceptional specimens possessing great antler and body size.

In addition, the high plains country east of the Continental Divide is becoming a whitetail hotspot. Specifically, these areas include the cottonwood drainages and subdrainages of the Missouri River. Its major subdrainages are the Jefferson, Gallatin, Madison, and Yellowstone Rivers. Much of the land is devoted to ranching and agriculture, although there are vast areas of high, rugged mountains contained in the Yellowstone and Missouri ecosystems.

Because elk and mule deer are exceptional trophies in their own right, the whitetail has often been overlooked in this region in the past. In recent years, natives of the region have begun to appreciate the magnificent qualities of the mountain and high plains whitetail — and this may well be the best-kept hunting secret in the United States. However, the popularity of trophy whitetail hunting in this region is on the upswing with interest coming from hunters in many different, more traditional whitetail hunting areas.

Let's look at some numbers. Montana ranks fifth in the top 10 states for numbers of Boone and Crockett typical and nontypical whitetails ever harvested. There have been 19 typical and 17 nontypical bucks taken. Idaho has a total of 6 bucks in the record book with two being typical and 4 nontypical. Montana has the Number 6 best typical head ever taken in North America. It was taken in 1974 and scored 199 3/8 points. (In order to qualify for minimum Boone and Crockett standing, a buck carrying a typical rack must score a minimum of 170 points, and one with nontypical antlers must score a minimum of 195 points. It is interesting to point out that almost half the bucks that rank in the top 10 lists in both typical and nontypical groups have been killed since 1971.) That is encouraging because it is well within the realm of possibility to take a "book" buck, even with today's hunting pressure.

Let's look at it this way. Wisconsin, at 68, has produced more total numbers of Boone and Crockett bucks than any other state. Montana and Idaho combined have produced a total of 42 Boone and Crockett bucks. Bear in mind, however, the total area containing viable whitetail populations in Montana and Idaho combined is smaller than that of Wisconsin. Also, whitetail hunting has been a way of life in Wisconsin since the mid-1800's. Many of the book heads were taken in the "good old days," while in the Northern Rockies, intensive whitetail hunting is a relatively new phenomenon.

Third, I want to share with you the exciting stories of how five great whitetails were hunted by men who know what they are doing — hunters like Gene and Barry Wensel, who prowl the mountains living and breathing whitetail deer every week of the year. By very carefully analyzing their stories and techniques, and reading between the lines, we can all become better sportsmen and more successful and satisfied whitetail hunters.

I must admit that I, too, am becoming more and more enamored with the magnificence of our native whitetail deer.

This text attempts to strike a balance between the meat hunter, the guy who wants to collect a respectable representative of the species, and the individual who accepts the supreme challenge of harvesting a buck whose antlers are large enough to earn a place in the Boone and Crockett listings. Thinking about it, the chapters perhaps tend to lean a bit toward the sportsman who wants to collect a larger than average specimen of the whitetail species. But that's fine because if the meat hunter employs 50 percent of the skill and knowledge required by big buck hunters, he will surely score.

All of the fine individuals who kindly related to me their hunting adventures and expertise are dedicated trophy hunters, so naturally the ideas put forth tend to flow in that direction. At my stage of hunting maturity, I tend to want to collect a more superior animal myself. I've paid my dues; long hours in tree-stands, bumbled opportunities, and season after season of collecting so-so bucks. Now, at age 43, I plainly and simply get more personal satisfaction passing up lesser bucks and trying to pit my hard-learned skills against a genetically superior animal.

After years of harvesting substandard bucks, I finally began to raise my standards.

I'll never forget the euphoric feeling I had when I was able to pass over a buck because I finally had the guts to raise my standards of acceptability. When the thrill of letting a younger, substandard buck walk away unharmed was greater than actually killing him, I knew I had moved one more rung up the ladder of hunting maturity and understanding.

Another way to make smaller racked bucks into acceptable trophies is to hunt them with a bow. I've done it and it is, pure and simple, fun. Bowhunting definitely puts the thrill back into whitetail hunting. Hunting deer with bow and arrow takes an entirely different psychological and hunting strategy. The rewards are great.

As the seasons rolled along, I found I got much more satisfaction and pleasure out of a hunt if the anticipatory parts of it were prolonged. The killing became less and less important. The sighting, stalk planning, stalking, choosing the best tree-stand sight, etc., became the heart and fun of a hunt. Don't misunderstand me, I still harvest deer gladly and enjoy my venison, but I think you know what I'm getting at.

I still gun hunt, too, but by being more selective much of the pre-hunt fun is preserved. Taking a typical buck that tops 160 or so Boone and Crockett points is no easy task. Gun hunting trophy-class bucks, like bowhunting any deer, will for sure rekindle interest in hunting whitetail.

Maybe we had best discuss what a trophy whitetail is. It is, of course, different things to different people. I definitely feel the trophy concept is directly related to the age of the hunter and or the number of deer kills he or she has under their belts.

My son, after taking his first deer this season, just about freaked out. I purposely watched his reactions immediately after the buck fell, curious to see what he would do. He bounced to his feet yelling, "Dad, dad, I got him!" His breath came in short, choppy gasps, and he wanted to run the 130 yards across the rocky draw that separated him from his prize.

To Scott, that buck (it was a good big-antlered breeding buck) was a trophy far better than the best buck ever killed. It was the reward of many trips to the gravel pit learning his rifle and five weeks of hard mountain hunting. The deer's antlers are mounted on an inscribed plaque and occupy a prominent place in our living room. Scott was 13 years old when he took that first buck, but a seasoned hunter looking for a top-heavy buck would have passed the deer over.

There are also individuals whose trophy is found in the freezer in the form of choice venison roasts, hamburger, and steaks.

There also are people whose hunting trophies are more intangible and have meaning only to themselves. A beautiful, crisp, clear, fall afternoon sitting by a pristine, murmuring stream lost in one's thoughts or feeling the rush of blood following good, hard exercise are trophies too. Taking a deer to these individuals is fine, but not taking one is okay too. To them the hunting experience has a deeper meaning than putting their tag on an antler.

A hunter's first buck is a great and noble trophy no matter what its size or species. This was the first deer my son, Scott, 13 at the time, harvested.

It is all in the mind of the doer and many of us will pass through all these stages as the years and experiences pile up.

Let me take a moment to summarize some conclusions I have reached after researching the literature and interviewing several whitetail fanatics. Then, upon reading the following pages, you can focus on the particular facet of whitetail hunting that interests you the most.

Hunters who are interested in collecting a trophy class buck are unanimous in their feelings about one thing — time. Weekend hunters rarely take exceptional bucks. The time must be spent in the woods before, during, and after the season. The sign must be studied and interpreted to learn the deer habits and a thorough understanding of the country hunted is necessary. Elk take physical stamina to harvest while

Learning the haunts and habits of a specific trophy animal, with the idea of taking only that individual deer, is a new approach to trophy hunting.

whitetail deer take mental alertness. It is a thinking game with whitetail deer. Thus, it stands to reason that the more trips made to the woods observing and studying sign, the better.

One obvious thought that is often overlooked for some reason is the fact that in order to harvest an above average buck, one has to hunt where there are such animals. Certain areas, including some entire states, don't have anything near trophy class bucks. It is foolish to hunt these places and expect to collect a good buck.

Another angle to big buck hunting that I learned from the Wensel brothers is to hunt a specific buck. This is sort of a new and radical idea I really hadn't considered. Not only do Gene and Barry hunt big buck areas, but they carry the idea one step farther and hunt a specific buck they have singled out. They lock in on a certain superior buck and learn everything they possibly can about him. Their hunt planning revolves around the movements and habits of that specific buck. They have raised the art of trophy hunting to new heights.

A deer's sense of smell never fails it. Human odor spoils more hunts than any single factor.

And finally, as with hunting elk, wind strength and direction are important considerations when hunting any deer, trophy or not. A deer's total world revolves around its ultra sensitive nose. Hunters who fail to watch and monitor the wind have little chance of collecting any deer except by sheer luck. A small feather or piece of frayed yarn tied to a bow limb or gun barrel will continually feed your brain wind information. Heed what it shows you.

Keep these four ideas in mind as you read on: spend time, learn an individual deer, hunt a big buck area, and monitor the wind constantly. Read between the lines and digest these thoughts carefully. Even if you have no desire to take a trophy, they will help you to harvest deer more consistently and enjoy the experience more.

Hole-in-the-Horn buck. It ultimately measured out as the fifth nontypical whitetail. This beautiful trophy languished in obscurity on a wall for decades before being rediscovered.

Chapter One

HISTORY OF WHITETAIL

During the last two decades, the popularity and recreational value of whitetail deer has exploded. The whitetail has gained many devoted fans, including me. One of the highlights of my day, every day, is observing numerous whitetail deer as I drive the last five miles between office and home. The road winds through a lightly populated mountain valley lined with alfalfa fields, cottonwood bottoms, and coniferous forests.

Does with twin fawns, groups of young bucks, and rutting bucks are all there at various periods during the year. They are all car tame and easily observed and studied. The experience is my daily high and sedative at the same time. I look forward to it, and I know that what I experience is duplicated throughout whitetail country.

The picture has not always been so rosy. Sixty years ago the whitetail population in most parts of North America was wiped out or greatly depleted. The whitetails' recovery has been nothing short of phenomenal. Even after having been eliminated from much of its historic range, the deer has recovered and even expanded its presence into areas that never before had a whitetail population. For any hunted mammal species to expand its historic range is an accomplishment almost unheard of. The coyote is the only other species hunted on a regular basis to do so to such a high degree.

In 1964, I began attending veterinary school in eastcentral Alabama. One of my professors was an avid quail hunter who spent many days each season afield. I think he had a secret desire to hunt deer, too, but the fact of the matter was there were no deer to speak of in that part of Alabama.

I remember clearly one day in 1966; he came to class all excited. He had seen a deer track while quail hunting that morning. If my memory serves me correctly, there was a productive deer season in east Alabama for the first time in anyone's memory the year I graduated in 1968. Today, Alabama's deer herd is in excess of 1.2 million animals — one of the biggest in the nation. The deer hunters in Alabama enjoy a long season and a very generous bag limit, a remarkable recovery but typical of many areas throughout the United States.

Whitetail deer have been studied and managed intensely during the last 30 years by the scientific community, probably more so than any other species in the world. The whitetails' recovery rests squarely on the shoulders of sportsmen-conservationists, dedicated wildlife biologists, and law enforcement officers who were and are willing to bear the costs and physical efforts involved. And, most importantly, the whitetail itself made that recovery possible by its ability to adapt a lifestyle to an ever-changing habitat.

Why were the vast numbers of deer existing at the time of our colonial ancestors exterminated from much of their original range? The answer makes an interesting story.

The whitetail were abundant in many different areas in North America, but their greatest numbers were found in coastal wetlands along the eastern seaboard and Gulf region. This was precisely where European man first set foot on the continent, and the destruction commenced.

Prior to the coming of European man, the deer was the staff of life to the eastern woodland tribes, much as the buffalo was to the Plains tribes. The Indian and deer lived a synergystic existence as the Indians harvested no more deer than was necessary to fulfill their seasonal needs. The deer benefitted in that numbers were kept in balance with their habitat.

It is estimated that approximately 2.34 million Indians lived within the inhabited range of the whitetail deer in precolonial times. By studying Indian village sites that were occupied continually for hundreds of years, it is possible to mathematically calculate the pounds of deer meat consumed per Indian per day. This figure is placed at an average of 1.5 pounds per individual per day. Further calculations show this to be about 427 million pounds annually. Then, by figuring the average yield of meat per deer, it can be surmised that 2.34 million Indians harvested 4.6 to 6.4 million whitetail deer per year.

Taking into account both animal predator losses and consumption due to native American (30 percent of total losses), deer populations would have to have been between 23.6 and 32.8 million over their total range in order to have sustained combined predator and Indian losses. For comparison, the present estimate of whitetail populations in North America stands at 14.2 million animals.

As a student and hunter of whitetail deer, it is interesting to note the ages of the deer taken by these aboriginal hunters during the time span

Today's whitetail herd in North America is approaching in total numbers that which is believed to have existed in pre-European days.

from 1000 B.C. to 1700 A.D. Dentition studies revealed the average age of harvested deer to be 3.5 to 4.5 years, somewhat older that the average age of deer harvested today. Sixty percent of the deer were harvested in winter and 43 percent were mature bucks.

After the mid-1600's, the North American natives quickly grew to covet the white man's steel tools and fire sticks. Likewise, the peoples of continental Europe grew fond of venison and finely-tanned buckskin. The skins were used to fashion soft, pliable garments and shoe linings. This new "export market" sealed the whitetails' fate — the natives no longer killed for subsistence but for profit. The deer were slaughtered by the hundreds of thousands.

Records show the rate of exportation of hides and meat from the New World to Europe. Between the years 1739 to 1765, 151,000 whitetail deer skins were shipped every year from Charleston, South Carolina, to England and Germany. An almost unbelievable 2 million pounds of deerskins and 600,000 deer carcasses left the port of Savannah, Georgia, bound for England during a 10-year period in the late 1700's. The situation was much the same in most of the colonies. The practice continued until about the year 1800. This type of pressure obviously couldn't go on too long before having considerable effect on the deer population.

Whitetail populations from 1800 until 1850 saw a temporary rebound in numbers. Two reasons were responsible for this. First, Indians had been

In colonial times deer were slaughtered in staggering numbers irregardless of age, sex, or time of year.

displanted, and their influence on whitetail numbers was greatly reduced. Second, the deerskin had lost prominence in the fur and hide trade.

This rebounding population was to later become the target of the market and pioneer subsistence hunters. This period extended from 1860 until 1910. Heavy pressure was again brought to bear on all forms of wildlife and nearly drove the whitetail to extinction.

This was a period of rapid expansion into and settlement of the western frontier. There were gangs of miners, railroaders, loggers, and settlers to feed. It was common practice for these groups to obtain meat directly from professional hunters or from township market places. Like contemporary man, our pioneer ancestors also enjoyed the luxuries of the period. These could be purchased with deer hides. Thus, the killing went beyond the needs of the stomach.

After the Civil War, the development of the repeating rifle and refrigerated rail cars accelerated the slaughter of wild game. Venison appeared on the menus of the finest restaurants in Chicago, New York, Boston, and Philadelphia. Hundreds of tons of venison were shipped each year to eastern markets to satisfy the demand. By the mid-1890's, the deer supply had dwindled and market hunting became less profitable.

The methods used by market hunters were varied, ingenious, and barbaric. Jacklighting with a shotgun loaded with buckshot was a favored method. Hunting from blinds, elevated platforms at mineral licks and runways, baiting with grain, running with hounds, pursuing in deep snow, snares, poison, deadfalls, set guns, and pitfalls were all methods used by the market hunter.

Newhouse, who perfected and manufactured leghold traps for small fur bearing mammals, even developed a leghold trap for deer — though he admitted then to it being "somewhat barbarous."

Early laws designed to protect deer were feebly enforced. They were usually a response to a temporary shortage of huntable deer and were soon forgotten. For instance, in 1646 Rhode Island prohibited deer hunting — the first recorded attempt to do so. The first colony to employ persons specifically to enforce game laws was Massachusetts. In 1739, that enforcement came — fully 40 years after the law had been enacted.

In 1900, the federal government, in response to demands from an increasingly conservation-minded public, passed a law called the Lacey Act which prohibited interstate trafficking in wild game taken in violation of state law. This gave great momentum to curtailing the steady decline of the whitetail by effectively ending market hunting.

In 1890, the U.S. Bureau of Biological Survey estimated that approximately 300,000 whitetail deer remained in the United States. Others estimated the census to be as high as 500,000. Whichever estimate was accurate is unimportant now. The point is that a near-fatal decline from the estimated precolonial numbers of 23 to 32 million animals had occurred.

To summarize some final thoughts: The whitetail at the turn of the century was a rarely hunted animal because it was rarely seen. Its recovery to present levels has been a remarkable event. Management, enforcement of game laws, improved habitat, and public awareness and outcry have all contributed to the whitetail's rebound.

By far the most important single factor in the whitetail's success story is the adaptability of the animal itself. It is one of the few large mammals that has adjusted to and even thrived in a habitat manipulated by man. Its ability to survive and prosper in close proximity to man is legend, and a key factor in its survivability.

Whitetail deer have adapted well to sparsely wooded, agricultural lands.

Chapter Two

CHARACTERISTICS AND HABITAT

There are 16 different subspecies of whitetail deer in the United States and Canada. Their population density is as high as 30 deer per square mile in central Texas and many states east of the Mississippi, to a low of 15 per square mile in the Northern Rockies.

The inhabited range of the whitetail deer is enormous and of incredible variety. Their range reaches from the Northwest Territories of Canada south throughout the length of Central America. They live in the salt marshes of Georgia and the coast forests of Washington and Oregon. In the Northern Rockies whitetail habitat is characterized by dense coniferous forests, wooded riverbottoms bordered by rangeland, or cultivated hay or grain fields.

Think about it. The diversity of vegetation types and differences in the whitetail's physical environment are almost unbelievable. I've hunted deer in the Everglades of south Florida where a sea of saw grass wetness stretches to the horizon and high ground is scarce. On the other hand, I've seen mature whitetail bucks running the subalpine environment on the ridge dividing Idaho and Montana near the head of Kelly Creek. The elevation was around 7,200 feet as compared to two feet in the Everglades.

Whitetails have developed special physical characteristics to cope with living continually in and around water. Their hooves are slender and pointed, much like a moose, to provide more support on soggy ground. Their hair coat is thin and short, even in winter, enabling them to better cope with a hot environment.

The air temperature variations alone that a Glades deer and a Rocky

Recently, big loner bucks have been spotted living in an alpine environment from 6,000 to 8,000 feet elevation.

The bogs, wet creek bottoms and swamps of the lowest elevations are tailor made for the secretive whitetail.

The subalpine forests of Douglas fir, lodgepole pine and ponderosa pine, interspersed with open parks and found west of the Continental Divide, make excellent whitetail habitat.

The whitetail's environment west of the Continental Divide is primarily open, dry and laced with creek bottoms, paralleled by narrow margins of brush.

Mountain whitetail must cope with will range from highs of 105 degrees in Florida to lows of minus 50 degrees (with no chill factor thrown in) in Montana. That's a differential of 155 degrees. Probably the only other mammal on this planet that can thrive in such variations of habitat and food types is man. But aren't we sportsmen lucky a whitetail is so adaptable physically? It is after all one of the keys to their dramatic increase in numbers in the last decade.

There are, however, large areas of some states which are void of whitetail deer. Western Colorado, New Mexico, and most of California, Nevada, and Utah are among them. Although whitetail deer are native to the mountains of Idaho and Montana, being found in abundance by trappers in the early 1800's, a very interesting development unfolding in the Northern Rockies has been the apparent rapid expansion of whitetail deer out of the cottonwood river and creek bottoms up into the higher mountains. For example, a friend of mine this past season took a very nice buck that was, as best as he could determine, living alone in a small basin at about 6,500 feet elevation. Although he was elk hunting, he located the buck bedded down in a dense patch of lodgepole pine and took him with a bow.

I personally had an interesting lesson in whitetail biology late last November. A buddy and I were hunting trophy mule deer in the Rattlesnake Wilderness in western Montana. The snow was above our knees, and the temperature was about 10 degrees Fahrenheit. We had been climbing higher all morning trying to reach the haunts of some really big muley bucks we knew to be in the area when I caught a flicker of motion ahead in the lodgepole. To my total surprise, a whitetail doe bounded away.

I often wish I had taken the time to backtrack her to see where she had come from. I'll never know if she was a transient or bedding and living in the area.

There is a real bonus to be had because of the current range expansion occurring with whitetail deer. The crescent shaped area encompassing large portions of British Columbia and Alberta, and arching down through Washington, Idaho, Montana, Wyoming, and thinning out down through portions of Colorado, Nebraska, Kansas, New Mexico, and Arizona has dual populations of whitetail and mule deer. We routinely hunt both species at the same time in the Northern Rockies, which adds an exciting dimension to our hunts.

The two species flourish on the same range, although studies showing how the habitat is shared or how the species interact are rudimentary. Whitetail deer and mule deer occasionally interbreed, producing a hybrid offspring. It is interesting to note there seem to be no areas in which the two species are ecologically separated in favored habitat types, except in cottonwood bottoms along creeks where it is unusual to find muleys.

Anatomically, there are three areas of interest to the whitetail connoisseur: the deer's external glandular structure and function, senses, and antler growth and development.

GLANDS

The glands are more developed and functional in bucks than in does and subsequent discussion will refer to bucks except for the interdigital glands.

Each gland, some more powerful than others, secretes a different odor or "pheromone" and these scents enable deer to communicate with each other. The odors can identify individual deer or indicate the stage of rut in the bucks. The exact triggering mechanism for release of glandular secretions are not fully understood. Probably involved are certain neurologic stimulation caused by shortened daylight hours plus physiologic changes taking place in does.

There are four external glands occurring in pairs and one singular gland. They are: the metatarsal glands on the outer surfaces of each rear leg located halfway between the hock and the hoof, the preorbital glands located in the inside corners of the eyes, the interdigital glands between the hooves, and most important, the tarsal glands occurring on the inner surface of each hock. The unpaired gland is called the forehead gland and is located in the skin of the forehead.

The forehead gland becomes active only during the rutting period. The breeding buck very carefully and deliberately rubs his forehead skin on a sapling as he alternates rubbing it with his antlers. Bucks evidently get great pleasure from the experience as they appear to be in an ecstatic state.

This imprints the buck's personal scent on the tree as a sign of his physiologic condition as well as identifying him individually to other bucks and does in the immediate area. The scent may last several days. Does can occasionally be seen smelling these forehead rubs.

The metatarsal glands on the outer surfaces of both rear legs serve limited function. They never reach the odiferous intensity of the tarsal glands but may serve to mark twigs and leaves as the deer moves through the brush.

The preorbital gland is best described anatomically as a deep fold or crease in the skin extending downward one to two inches below the inside corner of each eye. It is not as important a gland to the whitetail as it is to the elk. It serves to mark rubs and to imprint the buck's scent on leaves and twigs above a scrape. The buck does this by grabbing a small branch hanging over his scrape in his mouth then releasing the twig to spring back over his face.

The interdigital scent gland (between the toes) simply marks the deer's trail. They continually emit an odor year-round and don't become particularly active at any certain time of year. The odor is highly individualistic, enabling deer to identify each other sight unseen.

By far the most important glands in the breeding buck's arsenal are the paired tarsal glands located on the inside of each hock. They appear as dark patches of dense hair four to six inches in diameter. They too produce a scent unique to each individual deer.

An unusual behavioral pattern which is demonstrated by rutting bucks and associated with rubbing and scraping activity is the phenomenon of rub-urinating. A buck will spread his front legs slightly for balance and pull his back legs underneath his abdomen so his tarsal glands are touching. He then urinates downward over the glands as he rubs them together. The liquid mobilizes the glands' scent molecules and greatly increases the distance the odor carries. The liquid is then spread down the buck's rear legs, staining them with dark streaks and in some cases spilling on to the ground. By mixing with liquid (urine), the scent from the glands is spread over a larger area of the buck's body and more prone to be spread as advertising by wind currents. The odor is pungent and musky and can be detected by humans at considerable distances if the wind currents are right. The tarsal gland odor may serve to intimidate other bucks, but has other social functions including the attracting of does. Its full function is not fully understood.

One night, while walking home along a creek bottom after a hard day's hunt in the high country, I jumped an unseen critter at close range. After

The whitetail's paired tarsal glands are located on the inside surface of each hock. (Note the dark spot on the inside of this buck's right rear leg.) The gland is the buck's main communicating mechanism during the rut.

the crashing had died down, I proceeded down the trail and quickly had my nasal passages seared by a pungent musky odor. My nose identified the critter as a rutting whitetail buck. If this scent is detected it should bring you to full attention immediately and I'll guarantee you there is a mature breeding buck very close.

At any rate, the presence of numbers of highly developed, individualistic and superbly functional glands in whitetail deer indicate a complex social hierarchy and a patterned social structure. Scent signals among whitetail deer is a vital part of their communicating ability.

One other important source of olfactory communication in deer is urine. Urine odor will attract whitetail bucks to does in heat. Rising hormone levels, primarily estrogen, will physiologically change the doe. The rising estrogen levels signaling the beginning of estrus (heat) are influenced, especially in northern latitudes, by the length of day. The amount of light striking the retina of the eye triggers neuroendocrine mechanisms which in turn control the timing of the heat cycle.

Since the amount of available light varies very little from year to year, the breeding period will fall in the same narrow time frame every season. This will ensure the fawns are not born too early or late in the spring, thus avoiding extremes in weather conditions and subsequent fawn mortality.

Upon reaching estrus, the doe greatly increases her activity and, therefore, stimulates increased buck activity.

This pattern, however, changes in the southern areas of the United States with timing of the rut sometimes varying within relatively small areas. This may be a geographic species adaptation since the fawning period is not affected by inclement weather.

Upon approaching estrus, the doe becomes restless and increases nighttime activity. She urinates often. Odors found in the urine, also called pheromones, alert a breeding buck to her receptiveness. A doe will remain in heat 24 hours. If unfertilized after the first heat, a doe will repeat her heat cycle at 21 to 27 day intervals, sometimes through February or until she becomes pregnant.

What role does the buck's urine play? I've not been able to locate through a literature search definite researched evidence describing exactly what function buck urine does serve. I have found a few theories about what's going on and will report the ones that have surfaced most often and seem to me to be the most plausible.

A dominate buck will rub-urinate at random throughout its home range to intimidate other bucks.

A buck will frequently urinate into his scrapes, which then function as signposts to alert other deer of both sexes as to his dominance and breeding condition. It is thought that does will visit a urine-scented scrape and in turn leave their olfactory message through cross-urination. In other words, it is believed that during the rut deer of both sexes leave their own identification scents at the scrape site. This behavior has not been scientifically documented, but is generally accepted through observed behavior to be fact.

A buck, locating the scent of a doe at his scrape, is then able to determine her state of receptiveness and will track her by the indiviudalized scent of the interdigital gland between her hooves.

I have read two sources stating bucks probably attract a specific doe through pheromones in his urine deposited at a scrape. Let me outline noted hunter-author Gene Wensel's observations about the urine-doe-attraction theory as he stated it in his book *Hunting Rutting Whitetails*, and you can be the judge: "A buck will make a number of urine marked scrapes. These serve as bait so to speak for a doe approaching estrus. A doe selects a scrape which she cross-urinates. She has now conveyed her acceptance to a specific buck. She in effect creates a primary scrape or one where all the action is."

What Gene is saying is that when a doe nears ovulation and conditions are ideal, there must be a good buck-to-doe ratio for her to be able to select a specific buck. Thus she has the ability to choose her sire. In my opinion, this idea has credibility because cow elk, also members of the deer family, choose which bull breeds them provided the populations are well balanced.

The doe attempts to choose a healthy, vigorous buck. Wensel contends a difference in urine odor will key a doe to the health of a buck. Healthy bucks accumulate large amounts of body fat and pass excessive fat globules in the urine. Conversely, a buck in a poor state of health will be metabolizing muscle tissue. His urine has no fat content. Therefore, a doe will or will not cross urinate a buck's marked scrape depending on the urine odor of the buck. The buck then has no opportunity to detect the state of estrus in the doe if she elects not to cross-urinate.

It is safe to say that urine serves as an important means of communication between deer. It also functions as a social behavior regulator, especially during the breeding cycle. Much more controlled research needs to be done to draw definite conclusions. Interestingly, one door opened by research often exposes two or three more yet unopened ones.

SENSES

Eyesight plays an important part in a deer's ability to interpret its environment, but not as important as its nose or ears, at least in the context of interpreting danger and not everyday living activity.

The whitetail depends strongly on motion to locate and catalog an object. This is important for the hunter to remember. Walking in our quick, hurried human style is fine between hotspots, but deliberate, slow movements are a must at all times while actively hunting.

Most hunters learn quickly that whitetail deer most often fail to identify the hunter as a danger, provided the hunter is absolutely motionless and the wind is favorable. The deer fails in the majority of cases to recognize what it is seeing. Deer often will stare intently at the strange lump standing there but in due time generally relax and move on. However, one turn of the head or twitch of a human finger, and the hunter's game is all over.

Deer do have exceptional range of vision. They have a combination of monocular vision to each side (each eye can see different objects to its left and right at the same time) and binocular vision to the front. The structure of the eye socket and a large retina enable deer to see back along their flanks and behind them.

Deer also have two highly developed senses which must be acknowledged and understood by the sportsman. They are hearing and smell.

Nothing, and I reemphasize nothing, occurring in a whitetail's home range goes undetected. A deer knows every rock, tree, trail, scent pattern, and type of noise in its area.

What do I mean by type of noise in his area?

Whitetail deer, as we all know, have learned to live in man's "backpocket" so to speak. For example, just last week I was in a tree-stand overlooking a likely ambush spot not more than 300 yards from my front door. As time went by my ears were continually assaulted by an unbelievable array of obnoxious sounds. My soon-to-be neighbor was pounding and banging on his new home. The other neighbor started chainsawing his winter wood supply, and his son cranked up his three-wheeler. (I think it's time to move on up the canyon.)

Directly, a plump three-point whitetail buck came walking down the trail completely oblivious to the forementioned battery of sounds. The point: he had been hearing these things since he was a fawn and had become conditioned to accept that type of noise on a daily basis. It was catalogued as nonharmful in his memory bank. I call it a form of emotional adaptation.

Now what do you suppose would have happened if I had creaked a board on my tree-stand? The young buck immediately would have pulled the old disappearing act.

Of course a whitetail living away from human concentrations would react instantly to the beating of a hammer. It is not the type of sound he has learned to be nonharmful.

I've spent countless hours photographing and watching deer from tree-stands. Their ears are constantly working at a variety of angles. The ears instantly alert the deer's brain to an unusual or out-of-rhythm sound such as the walking of human feet. These sounds are quickly sorted out and reacted to either in a negative or positive way.

While deer depend on their eyes to detect motion, their most highly developed senses are those of smell and hearing.

By far the deer's most powerful defensive sense is its nose. With its nose, the deer interprets and makes judgments on everything in its environment; odors never lie. A deer's eyes will often fail him and sometimes his ears — but never his nose. A twig snapped under a still hunter's foot will be soon forgotten because other residents of the deer's world are always snapping twigs. But there is only one thing that can bring man scent to a deer, and that is man himself. There is no other smell like it in the deer's natural world.

The deer's nose is never turned off. The process of exhaling and inhaling to maintain life constantly brings a flow of information to be interpreted and acted upon.

My thirteen-year-old son, Scott, already a successful deer hunter, got his first real experience with man-scent problems just this week. Here in western Montana we are in the process of enjoying a prolonged deer season in one area. The regular season has been extended to curtail a rapidly expanding whitetail population in the Montana's Bitterroot Valley.

We were laying near a haystack overlooking a small gully through which the deer were funneling to get to the cut-over alfalfa fields and hay stacks. The temperature was minus 2 degrees, and we were beginning to stiffen pretty good when about 30 does and fawns came pouring out of the sagebrush, heading for the gully at a trot. I'm sure they had visions of tender, succulent alfalfa tips dancing in their heads.

Scott tensed as I nudged him our prearranged signal to get ready to shoot. The plumes of steamy breath we exhaled had been flowing nicely over our shoulders when suddenly the wind changed, reversing its flow. A chorus of foot stomps and nasal snorts immediately greeted us. Scott whispered, "Dad, what's happening?" He had just received his initial, firsthand experience with the power of a deer's nose and the fickleness of wind direction.

Let me relate an instance passed on to me by a friend in which whitetails used their noses to modify their behavior to adapt to a particular situation.

A farmer named Hansen had a modest beef operation but a not so modest deer population running his small acreage. The deer soon learned to hang around the barn and dine on the grain and hay leftovers. Almost every evening Hansen would walk past the deer as he returned to the house after completing feeding chores. The deer and the farmer had developed a kind of mutual acceptance.

One day a hunter got permission from Hansen to hunt his farm with a bow. Hansen told the hunter the deer were not very man shy and to set up by the barn in the evenings near where Hansen walked home after feeding. Hansen said he would have no trouble getting his deer.

The hunter had no success. The deer were very wary and wouldn't come in. Why? The deer had obviously become comfortable with Hansen's evening routine and his mannerisms. They had apparently learned to identify his particular scent, tainted heavily as it was with cow manure, as nonharmful. Gee, I wonder if some entrepreneur might come up with bottled cow and hog manure scent. But then my wife would make me leave my clothes hanging outside in a tree!

The project was carried one step farther. The prevailing winds and Hansen's work routine were such that his scent was almost always blowing to the deer. At my friend's suggestion, one day Hansen changed the direction from which he returned to his home from the barn. The wind now blew from the deer to Hansen. You guessed it; the deer abruptly fled.

Never underestimate the behavioral adaptation ability of contemporary whitetail deer. Their bag of tricks is deep, and anything can happen.

I'm going to take the liberty at this point to invent another sense, one that is highly developed and can often be used by the observant outdoorsman to collect a trophy. In my opinion it ranks along with the nose as a deer's first line of defense. It is also as important as glandular secretions for a communicating media among deer. It is called body language.

Deer show dominance, intimidation, breeding status, excitement, fear, etc., by changing the position of their limbs, ears, head, and body. They

A breeding buck displaying breeding posture. Its head and neck are extended and carried low while its ears flop along its neck. This body attitude is demonstrated when close to a doe in estrus.

are continually showing their reactions to other deer and to man. Since deer are often in groups or in visual contact with other deer, they depend on each other to multiply their watchfulness. Every deer can depend on the reactions of others to help read its environment.

Let's say we are in a high tree-stand and essentially invisible to detection by deer. It is November 20 and the rut is in full swing. The tree-stand is located over the corner of a small alfalfa field that the deer are using heavily. It's about 30 minutes before dark. You see a large solitary doe cautiously approach the hay meadow.

She pauses a few yards inside the swamp before leaving its security and gazes intently into every corner of the field. Her sensitive ears are rotated forward, listening. She holds her stare for several minutes while working her nose up and down. She shows no overt signs of detecting a human. Her empty belly tells her to hurry.

Suddenly, still peering forward, one ear is rotated backward, listening. She's telling us there are more does and fawns trailing behind. She knows they are coming and is checking their progress. She is also sending signs by her reactions that the coast is clear. "Let's eat!"

Gingerly, the dominant lead doe steps into the field, eyes and ears at full alert. Her body motion is calculated, direct and cautious, but not alarmed. Quickly she relaxes and begins to feed. In short order, eight does, fawns, and a single forkhorn step into the clearing without so much as a pause and begin to feed.

A dominance posture is demonstrated by an erect head and neck, ears flared forward and an intense stare. Note that the less dominant buck carries his head and neck lower and ears are back. He demonstrates a submissive posture.

After a few minutes of observation, the group's pecking order begins to unfold. On the bottom are the doe fawns, who are driven out of choice feeding spots by all the other deer, even buck fawns. The dominant animal lays its ears back along its neck and may step forward and strike the weaker individual with a front hoof. The less dominant animal will crouch down, tuck its tail, drop its ears, and slink off a few feet. Confrontation over.

Undetected, we watch as one or another of the deer briefly raise their heads from feeding to check the surroundings. A doe's head jerks erect at an unseen signal and she stares, not a casual checking glance, but a serious, hard look. The other deer instantly see her concern and are alerted. Stiff posture, erect head and neck, intense staring spell trouble. The deer stare at the alarmed doe to read her reactions. They don't look where she is looking.

She raises a front foot and stomps the ground, showing a higher level of concern. The other deer begin to mill about nervously, some with tails erect. We follow the deer's stare and see a coyote trotting off into the timber. The doe relaxes and begins to feed, disalarming the rest of the group.

As darkness creeps across the meadow, the dominant doe stares past our stand into the swamp. Her look is fixed with ears forward, but her body is not stiffened with alarm. The herd stares at her for more signals.

A buck carrying a heavy five-point rack, detecting no alarm in the does, moves quickly toward them. His well-muscled body and confident attitude set him apart. His motion causes all eyes to lock on him. He lays back his ears and swaggers into the herd, causing the younger animals, including the forkhorn, to squat and sulk out of his way.

The mature, older does are more reluctant to yield as he checks them for signs of estrus. He moves from one to another smelling, checking, and bullying.

As if on cue, three of the adult animals are at attention, looking into the darkness at the far end of the meadow. "What's happening," we wonder. We haven't seen or heard anything. The wind is good.

The deer are agitated; their tails are up. Fawns are looking to their mothers for their next move. From across the hay meadow a shrill nasal whistle splits the night air. We have been winded by an unseen deer. Pandemonium — waving tails and flying snow. The does break hard for the swamp. We notice the buck slipping away in an opposite direction while keeping a low profile and his tail down. He escapes quickly.

The reason for this short story is to get you to think about "reading" deer. They can give you a tremendous amount of useful information about what their mental state is. This recognition will come with experience and your tactics and plans can be adjusted, oftentimes at the last minute, to enable you to fill your tag.

One final thought must be mentioned concerning a deer's so-called sixth sense or its incredible ability to feel danger even though it's not sure why. I'm absolutely convinced that many times when a deer seems to do some sort of strange behavior or some elusive maneuver, however subtle it may be, it is really because it is reading another deer which has seen you, but you don't know is around.

We have all had a buck that was coming in nicely, completely oblivious to our presence, suddenly stop, its attitude alert. He will turn his head from side to side, looking and listening for several seconds, and suddenly turn and walk in the opposite direction. He's not in a panic, but something in his mind wasn't just right.

Deer have a very complex, sophisticated means of communicating with each other. Their techniques are as intricate as our spoken language. I feel the biologists have barely begun to understand the many facets of whitetail communication.

ANTLERS

A buck's antlers are composed of pure bone. Their development starts in April and is fully completed by early August. By September, the antlers are hard and firm and much of the velvet has been removed.

The stages of development are controlled by a hormone called testosterone. If the source of testosterone is removed by castration, the buck will shed his hardened antlers within a week. Under a normal situation, in mid-January the supply of testosterone decreases forming a separation layer at the skull pedicle, and the antlers fall off. With adequate nutrition, especially protein, it is possible for some bucks to retain their antlers until early March.

The size of a buck's antlers are dependent on three things: nutrition intake and quality, genes, and age of the deer. A major reason why many whitetail areas in the United States produce poor quality racks is because the average age of a harvested deer is 2 1/2 years. They are just babies, not having matured in body size or antler development. This is why there are so many big, heavy racked whitetail bucks in the Northern Rockies. They simply are not hunted with intense pressure.

A well-balanced herd is one in which the herd's range is not over-burdened by large numbers of deer and has not reached maximum carrying capacity. Forage quality should remain high provided it was high to begin with. However, a buck with poor genetic make up will never have a superior set of antlers no matter what type of food is available or how many years he lives. Conversely, a buck with superior genetic structure will never grow a trophy rack on a poor supply of nutrition or if he is killed at a young age.

Record class animals must be born genetically superior, have access to highly nutritious forage, and live to be at least 5 1/2 to 8 1/2 years of age. There are many places close to my hometown of Missoula, Montana, where such circumstances are all present.

As a six-month animal, a buck will have buttons or small knobs where his antlers will grow. As a 1 1/2 year old and growing his first rack, the buck's genetics and nutrition will begin to influence antler development. For example, it has been proven beyond any doubt that a spike buck is genetically deficient and will only grow longer spikes or at most a spindly forkhorn or three-point rack. He will never grow trophy class antlers. On the other hand, a 1 1/2 year old buck with forked or three or four points on his rack (western count) will someday, given time and proper diet, be a superior animal.

Just this past season, I was bowhunting during the rut on a ranch managed by a friend of mine. For the last several years he has been culling inferior bucks, strictly regulating the deer harvest, and improving habitat. As a result, I watched a 1 1/2 year old buck with a perfect, symmetrical four-point rack feed under my tree stand. He had one-half-inch

Under normal conditions, decreasing levels of testosterone causes the formation of a separation layer at the pedical of the antler, and they are shed. This occurs anytime during late September through mid-February.

brow tines and three small points on each slender antler. His small body, slender neck, and immature facial features told me he was a youngster.

A buck reaches full sexual maturity, antler development, and body size at about 6 1/2 to 8 1/2 years of age. He then begins to slide downhill. At 10 1/2 to 12 1/2 years of age, he is an "old man" in poor physical condition and with a degenerated rack.

Let's take a look at the Boone and Crockett Club and its listing of whitetail trophies.

The club is an organization founded in January 1888 by Theodore Roosevelt and is dedicated to the written recognition of trophy specimens of North American big game. The animals are listed in the club's official publication, called *Records of North American Big Game.* Copies of this book are available from the Boone and Crockett Club, 205 South Patrick St., Alexandria, VA 22314. The cost of the current edition is $29.95 plus $2.00 shipping.

The odds against taking a record buck are staggering. Some estimates put the figure at one buck per one million harvested or .000001 percent. Many of the top whitetail experts think the minimum scores required to make the book (170 typical points and 195 nontypical points) are ridiculously high.

The Boone and Crockett scoring system gives credit in four major areas. Total beam and tine length account for roughly 70 percent of the score. Eighteen percent goes to massiveness or thickness of the antlers and 12 percent of the score is allotted to inside spread at the widest point. Symmetry of each antler as related to its mate is also considered. Abnormal points and differences in the overall measurements of one antler to the other are deducted from the total score.

All things considered, if a rack is weak in any scoring area, points must be made up in other places. Since most of the score is credited to the aggregate length of the main beams and their points, "book" buck cannot be deficient in this category. Massiveness and spread don't count enough to make up too great a beam and tine length deficiency.

A superior rack will have main beams with a length of between 26 and 28 inches. The inside spread will be between 20 and 24 inches. There will be 12 to 14 total points, and an antler base between the burr and first point that is 4 7/8 to 5 5/8 inches around.

I've heard it stated, "If you have any question whether or not the buck you're looking at is a Boone and Crockett class animal, forget it." When and if you are lucky enough to see one, you will know — period! The sight will literally take your breath away.

I'll never forget the first real trophy class buck I saw a few years ago. I was in a tree-stand positioned in a small ponderosa pine grove and was attempting to collect deer photos. A single doe wandered toward my stand but was still about 50 yards away when I caught a slight motion out of the corner of my eye. I could see the body of a second deer whose head was hidden behind a large ponderosa. Both deer stood motionless for several minutes, facing each other. Even though it was mid-December, I felt certain the doe was unsettled and was in her second heat cycle. That meant, hopefully, that the deer with the hidden head was a buck.

Finally, it stepped clear and, honestly, I just sucked in my breath in amazement. The buck's rack was so wide and tall I thought at first he had a deformed head. It looked shrunken. He was a tremendous example of a whitetail buck. I knew instantly he was "book" material.

He chased off the doe, and I only managed to get long range pictures, which were subsequently enlarged to 16 by 20 inch size and examined by Gene Wensel and Dick Idol. Both proclaimed the buck to be one of the biggest bucks ever photographed alive in the wild. The memory of that buck is still very vivid in my mind. Incidentally, I've checked extensively and as far as I know, that buck has never been seen again or harvested. (Later that year both of the buck's shed antlers were found and calculating average spread, minus a few deducts, he scored 183 Boone and Crockett points.)

What is a typical rack? It is one which can have up to eight normal points on each antler. The tines must originate from the main beam in a straight up position. Typical antlers usually are symmetrical or nearly so meaning the left antler closely resembles the right antler in size, conformation, and number of points. Sometimes typical antlers will have minor abnormal points and still be considered typical. These points will be subtracted from the total score.

A nontypical rack is a pair of antlers that deviates from the general eight symmetrical points per side seen on a typical rack. It can have a large number of points originating from an abnormal location on the main beam or from any position on other points. The main beam and point arrangements can on some occasions be very exotic.

There are a total of 769 typical and nontypical whitetail bucks listed in the 8th edition (1981) of the Boone and Crockett record book. There are 456 typical bucks and 313 nontypical bucks listed. The largest typical buck scored 206 1/8 points and was killed in Wisconsin in 1914. (There is now under Boone and Crockett consideration, a buck which was taken in 1983 in Saskatchewan, Canada and scored 204 6/8 points. It would become the new number three typical in the world.) The largest nontypical buck listed scored at 286 points and was killed in Texas in 1892. (A new candidate for the new world record nontypical whitetail buck was found dead in St. Louis County, Missouri. The antlers scored 325 7/8 points. It shattered the 90 year old nontypical record for the number one position by nearly 40 points.) One hundred seventeen bucks ranked in the typical category were killed between 1970 and 1979 while 83 nontypicals were killed between 1970 and 1979.

SPECIAL CONSIDERATIONS

The Rocky Mountain whitetail must cope with an extremely harsh winter climate. Deep crusted snow and subzero temperatures can persist for days and even weeks at a stretch. Since the whitetail as a species is a very hardy and resourceful animal, they cope well provided there is adequate nutrition available.

During the tough winter months, the whitetail will take advantage of whatever habitat type is found in its home range. In mild winters in northwest Montana and northern Idaho, deer tend to concentrate in shrubbed-over logging areas or burns. They must, however, have secure cover close by to utilize such areas. Extensive clearcuts prohibit use by deer.

In central and westcentral Montana, the lower mountain slopes are blanketed by open parks surrounded by stands of ponderosa pine and other coniferous species. The pines then yield, at lower elevations, to agricultural lands. In severe winters the deer will bed in the stands of timber and descend to the the alfalfa fields to feed.

Severe winters in the Kalispell-Glacier Park region of northwest Montana cause the deer to seek dense, mature spruce stands to escape snow

Searching the woods for sheds is a good scouting technique showing the number, size and distribution of bucks in an area. The white shed is a year older than the fresh shed on the right.

depths of more than 22 inches in the open. These protected sites are selected close to feeding areas, if possible, and the deer then make daily movements, single-file, along well beaten paths to their feeding area.

As with elk, availability of quality food supplies is critical to the well being of whitetail deer in the Northern Rockies. Since these wintering areas are at low elevations, the deer face the inevitable conflict with human activity. Harassment and killing of deer by domestic dogs has been and continues to be a major problem in certain areas. Deep snow, with or without a crust, complicates the dog problems.

To conserve valuable energy, the deer become very sedentary, almost going into a stupor during the tough months of December, January, and February. Movements are limited to moving between bedding and feeding areas. Their dense winter coats trap tiny pockets of air which the body heats. The heated air insulates them against the bone-numbing cold.

These are some of the behavioral and physiologic adaptations which protect the animals against harsh winters. If the winter is prolonged with deep snow, a die off may occur.

Whitetail deer are thought to be browsers but in reality, they consume a variety of food types. grasses, fruits, forbs, mushrooms, wood-type shrubs,tree parts-cottonwood, aspen, western cedar, and Douglas fir are preferred types, and various types of agricultural crops. Like elk, whitetail deer have the ability to select and eat the types of plant materials which are most nutritious. This choice of prime foods enable deer to better survive under difficult conditions.

Food preference during hard times is influenced by availability. Deer will consume any type of plant available, despite its palatability, if survival depends on it. If deer are forced to consume high volume, high fiber type forages during crisis periods, the physical size of the digestive track will limit the amount of food taken in. Winter-killed deer that have starved will sometimes have a rumen full of plant matter that is of a coarse, low quality and unable to provide adequate calories and protein to survive.

For a long time it was believed that whitetail deer had a very small, one-square-mile home range. It is now understood that a rutting buck will stray as far as eight to ten miles from his home range. He does this mostly after dark, takes no unnecessary chances, and returns home quickly. His home range is where he will spend the majority of his life. In it he will have all of life's necessities-water, food, and adequate security cover. Whitetail deer tend to use the same home range year after year unless some major disturbance such as a subdivision development forces them away.

HOME RANGE FACTORS

Whitetail deer maintain a small home range while mule deer live over vast acreages. By doing so, the whitetail gains a major survival advantage. They become intimately familiar with every aspect of their home range and can immediately identify an object or smell that is out of place. Mule deer therefore are more vulnerable because of range unfamiliarity and consequently suffer higher hunter mortality.

The shape of the whitetail's home range is usually elliptical. A range thus shaped enables the deer to become familiar with an area that can provide the maximum amount of cover and vegetation types with a minimum of movement and exposure. Adult bucks usually have a larger basic home range than do does.

Within a whitetail deer's home range will be an area where they spend the majority of their daylight hours. This can be thought of as the "core area" of that home range. Bucks particularly select the areas of densest cover for these secret hideouts.

Deer tend to use one portion of their home range during the night (feeding area) and another during the day (bedding areas). Oftentimes they have night bedding sites which are in or near the food source. Deer in mountainous terrain tend to bed high during the day and move into lower areas at night to feed. Whitetails usually remain bedded for no more than two hours at a time.

An example occurred on a hunt I had in Montana's Bitterroot Valley a number of years ago. About 2:30 in the afternoon, I picked up several sets of deer tracks leading toward the head of a large, rocky, open sagebrush draw. Mingled with the line of smaller tracks were the prints of a larger deer. Since the rut was on, I figured the large tracks were pro-bably a buck following a group of does.

Being intimately familiar with the country, I cut over into an adjoining draw to get ahead of and above where I thought the deer to be headed. I knew the country held super bucks so I was excited.

Peering over the top, I saw six or eight does ambling up the draw. Shortly, I spied the buck sniffing along behind. He was good, not exceptional — a nice five-pointer. I watched the bunch to await developments and set a game plan. Surprisingly, the buck ambled away from the does up the opposite side of the draw and bedded directly across from my position on about the same level, about 275 yards away. The does continued on out of the draw, passing about 30 yards to my left through a small saddle. It was just me and the buck.

I hunkered down just off the rim of the draw where I could lay and study the buck. I was screened from his view by a thin veil of grass. My plan was to sit tight, thinking the buck would shortly get up and follow the does. I shoot an iron sighted pre 64 Model 70 .270 Winchester and prefer my shots much closer if possible. A stalk was impractical as the draw was wide open covered with short sagebrush scrub.

I decided to wait until the sun was just beginning to touch the Bitterroot Range to my back for the buck to make his move. If forced to shoot from where I was, I wanted to leave a little tracking light just in case. It was 3:15 p.m.

At 4:20, the buck stood up and I readied myself. Well, the old boy stretched mightily, urinated, turned around, and laid back down.

I glanced toward the sun. It was decision time. I thought about mimicking a bear and crawling in full view, on all fours, diagonally toward the buck, hoping he might hold long enough for me to close down the range.

Pulling out my binoculars, I studied the buck carefully. He was bedded looking slightly downhill. A small bush screened only his face. He was unaware of any human presence and appeared settled in for a while. It was a tough shot for me as I rarely shoot at that range. I decided to go for it as my only practical course of action. Placing my daypack in front of me, I laid my rifle across it. I was steady, having rested a long time.

The front bead of my rifle completely filled the deer's chest areas so I made several dry runs looking over the sights. Damn, he was small! I let out half a breath, felt steady and squeezed off. The deer looked like he had spring-loaded legs; he rocketed out of his bed and shot down the draw at a gallop.

As he ran, I got into a sitting position and chambered another round. Just then he stopped suddenly and looked down the draw away from me, obviously confused as to where the shot had come from. I drew careful aim. He was facing obliquely downhill. I touched off and the buck reared on his hind legs and did a backward summersault. He righted himself and was pulling himself along on his front legs. After about 10 seconds he fell heavily to his side and was still.

After examining the buck, I discovered his spine was shattered just

Unlike elk and mule deer, whitetail deer live and thrive in close proximity to man, including man's machines and dogs.

behind his ribs. He had died within seconds of being hit. He scored 148 Boone and Crockett points.

Since there are marked seasonal differences in the vastness of the northern Rocky Mountains, deer in some localities have a modest migration cycle, a summer and winter range so to speak. The migration patterns of whitetail deer don't approach the grand scale of mule deer or elk, which may change entire habitat types and move many horizontal miles.

In Montana, migrations of up to 9 to 25 miles have been reported, but most movements are shorter and most likely to involve vertical distance rather than horizontal distance. Migration patterns are usually not a factor while hunting deer in the Northern Rockies.

Migrations generally are triggered by cold weather accompanied by deep snow. Snow depths of about shoulder height seriously impede a deer's movements as well as making feeding more difficult.

Today's whitetail, particularly the older, trophy-type bucks, have developed unique and sometimes complicated strategies that allow them to thrive in a wide variety of habitats and in extremely close proximity to man and his machinery. Even if forced to vacate an area because of intense human pressure, they soon return to re-inhabit old territory once the human activity has moderated.

In summary, whitetail deer are able to survive intense hunting pressure and competition with man for habitat on all fronts. They are not forced out of their home ranges by a density of one hunter to 10 acres although they may temporarily modify daily movement cycles. Their range includes wider variations in climate and geography than any other big game species in the world.

Paul Brunner shows a buck which scored 183 B&C points after deductions. The buck is very heavy beamed with long tines.

Chapter Three

MANAGEMENT AND POPULATION DYNAMICS

The roots of wildlife management theory first appeared in the late 1800's. It was determined through a test court case that states hold ownership of the wild game populations and not individuals. Since this was true, it was also determined later, again through court proceedings, that this right of ownership also embodied the states with police powers to manage and protect wildlife for the people.

This whole concept was a radical departure from the way wildlife was managed in Europe. There the game was owned and zealously guarded by the owner of the estate on which the game lived. The common man simply had no access to the game.

What is the need for deer management in the first place? Whitetail deer are very prolific. (With minimum mortality and optimum food and cover, the reproductive rate of whitetails could double their numbers every year or two.) They maintain a high profile to the general public because they live so intimately with man. Also, the whitetail deer is a highly prized and valuable recreational resource to the hunter and wildlife watcher alike.

The economic value of the whitetail is staggering — transportation, license fees, food, lodging, equipment, and the list goes on and on.

I wonder, too, about the intangible and immeasurable value hunting deer has toward the development and maturation processes of young minds and bodies. And we also need to consider the emotional relief enjoyed by millions of men and women while slipping through the woods.

The value of firm, lifetime bonds developed between parent and child while hunting are incalculable. The experience my son and I shared when he took his first deer this season can't be measured in words. It was his second season of hard mountain hunting and, though discouraged, he stuck with it and took a big mule deer buck 20 minutes after daylight on a beautiful, cold, sunny day high in a mountain park. The stalk and positioning ourselves for the shot took about 30 minutes of teamwork. It was a very rewarding experience for us both and will never be forgotten. I wonder in what subtle or dramatic way this has influenced Scott's life and how later will it manifest itself in his personality.

Our experience and thousands of others like them are possible only because of wildlife management principles enforced by state and federal game agencies and the foresight of our ancestors who demanded such policies.

State agencies must balance management policies to provide the most good for the most people — hunting and nonhunting public alike. Decisions have to be tempered toward the preservation of the environment, too. Despite what some groups feel, hunting is and must continue to be the main tool used to maintain physically strong whitetail herds and a healthy environment.

Unfortunately, important management decisions are frequently influenced by so-called biopolitics. Special interest groups with a strong lobby can prevent management decision being made in the best interest of the deer or the general public.

If wildlife is to be held in public trust by the states, we're still unclear as to who does the managing. At the federal level, agencies such as U.S. Forest Service, Fish and Wildlife Service and the Bureau of Land Management administer policies set by the legislative and executive branches of government. At the state level, commissions or boards appointed by the governor formulate policy. Input is given to the commissions from state game biologists, private organizations such as rod and gun clubs or a state bowhunters association, and private citizens.

Whitetail management could fundamentally be defined as keeping deer numbers in balance with themselves and their habitat by some form of removal. New additions must be balanced by a mortality in the existing population. In the absence of natural predators such as the wolf and cougar, hunting becomes the most efficient, workable solution for keeping an expanding deer population in a proper balance with the habitat.

The antihunting and preservationist groups evidently don't buy that idea and I truly feel sad about their well-intentioned but misinformed feelings.

When a deer is born it will some day die from one cause or another. There are several alternatives. A deer herd can overgraze its range and many of them will starve. I doubt the antis have the foggiest idea what it is like to starve to death. I haven't suffered the misfortune myself but have, on numerous occasions, seen deer and elk that were walking skeletons and in considerable discomfort. Starvation isn't quick nor is it pretty. If a starving deer is lucky a predator or internal parasites will give the doomed critter a quicker, more merciful death.

Mounted sheds recovered off a well-managed whitetail range in the Northern Rockies. These two bucks have all the ingredients — mass, tine length, and spread.

Let's say a deer is on good range and simply gets old. Invariably the incisor teeth become worn, loose, and fall out. The molars become flat and table-smooth and the deer becomes unable to chew the rough forage plants. This deer also starves slowly as he becomes less and less able to nip off and chew buds and stems.

A too-large deer herd living in suburban America has increased exposure to man's best friend, dogs. I'll bet the preservationists have never seen a dog pack pull down a doe and eat her intestines while she is still alive. Again, it is not a nice sight.

It seems to me that being shot and killed quickly and perhaps with a brief moment of pain is clearly a more humane choice. Oh, I can hear the screaming now about all the wounded and suffering animals. It's kind of like our government. On occasion some laws and rules that maintain a workable, livable society hurt certain individuals but improve the quality of life for the majority. Case rested!

Population dynamics of any segment of a wildlife population is influenced by three factors — death, replacement, and shifts in population concentrations. All three must be in balance to have a vigorous whitetail herd. Even if death and replacement are in balance, a movement of deer from one region to another can cause problems. Relocation of a population occurs because of an undesirable situation occurring in the home range or a more desirable habitat attracting deer to a different location.

By using harvest techniques plus good range management, Paul Brunner is now seeing bucks like this on his ranch. This buck is only 2 1/2 years old and sporting only his second rack — but note that it is large and very symmetrical.

For example, in 1982 south Florida received unusual amounts of rainfall. The high water levels decreased the deer's livable habitat by 95 percent. Too many deer were competing for the very limited food resource. Because of the slow nature by which excess water is drained away, the state game department planned a special hunt to reduce the herd by 5,000 animals. The animals were not only starving — they were doing irreparable damage to the habitat resource.

The antihunting crowd failed to see the logic in such a hunt and went to court to stop it. They argued, somewhat successfully, to be permitted to attempt to "rescue" and relocate the starving deer. A compromise was reached and the antis were permitted to capture deer for relocation from a part of the proposed hunting area. After succeeding in capturing only 18 animals the preservationists conceded the task impossible. Only seven of the captured deer survived the handling and relocation.

It appears the segment of the public which have a grasp of the principle of wildlife management and population dynamics are having a hard time convincing the general public of the importance of sound, ethical wildlife management ideas. This is perhaps a little easier to understand when it is realized that 80 percent of the American people don't hunt. It must be mentioned that most of these people are not anti-hunters.

After all the dust has cleared and the chest-beating subsides, there are really only two considerations when managing whitetail deer. They are population control and habitat management — and the two cannot be separated.

POPULATION MANAGEMENT

Numbers of deer are managed most efficiently by regulated harvests. Controls must be set by state game commissions that are flexible enough to take into account slow-occurring trend differences in population structure or habitat alterations. Agencies must be able to respond to acute, short-term problems such as the one which occurred in the Everglades, and which occur elsewhere on a continuing basis. Another example of a short-term but serious problem is the destruction of domestic stock feeds which occurs in Montana's Bitterroot Valley every December, January, and February. The Montana Department of Fish, Wildlife and Parks responds to this problem each winter by conducting a generous, extended archery season which can last through mid-February. Season lengths, opening and closing dates of hunting seasons, numbers of licenses issued, sex and ages of deer to be harvested in a management unit are all used as means of controlling deer numbers.

The total whitetail population in a given area can be increased by having a buck only harvest. However, the number and quality of bucks taken will decrease as their age structure becomes younger due to over harvest.

Overall deer numbers can be decreased by harvesting does and bucks.

Since some hunters in this situation will be satisfied to fill their tags with a doe, less overall pressure will be exerted on the buck segment of the herd. Therefore, some bucks will live longer and have a chance to grow bigger, heavier antlers. Taking this scenario a step farther, if a harvest limit were placed on the age classes and numbers of bucks bagged some real trophies would appear in a few years provided the nutrition level was good and the genetic structure sound.

This is precisely what many ranches are doing in Texas where deer are looked upon as a cash crop. Many of these ranches are very large and enclosed with deer-proof fences, making possible very strict controls over the types and numbers of bucks taken. The hunts are planned and coordinated in many cases by a professional game biologist. Hunters pay a stiff fee for the privilege of having a chance to take a good buck produced under an ideal management situation.

Obviously, this type of situation is more difficult to produce in the Northern Rockies — and it is unnecessary. Management of whitetail deer is almost totally done by setting hunting and licensing regulations by the state game agencies. No restrictions are placed on the sizes of bucks taken. In Montana for several years now, there has been an attempt to control the overall population by permitting does to be harvested the first three days of the general rifle season and during the entire archery season. As discussed before, this will have a bearing on the numbers of bucks harvested.

It's a shame this young buck, with such great potential, was harvested.

Many hunters would not go afield unless the opportunity to take a doe was there. Knowing that harvesting a doe is almost a sure thing, many marginal or weekend sportsmen are thus encouraged to hunt. This is valuable to the overall management picture because the herd size is checked taking pressure off the habitat.

Actually, this situation, outside of fenced Texas-type controlled ranches, probably goes farthest toward satisfying the most people. Bucks have time to survive long enough to grow big racks for the trophy hunter yet the meat hunter has ample opportunity and sufficient population of deer to satisfy his needs.

HABITAT MANAGEMENT

In Texas, where some lands are reserved primarily for growing maximum sizes and numbers of deer, habitat management is a big factor influencing the quality and size of the deer herd. Again, being in a controlled situation on a set piece of real estate makes aggressive habitat manipulation feasible. To my knowledge, there is only one ranch in the Northern Rockies that is managed strictly for the growing of trophy bucks. This ranch and its owner will be examined more closely elsewhere in this book.

In the Northern Rockies, the whitetail habitat is managed mainly through control of the deer herd. Browse quality and quantity are controlled by limiting the numbers of deer themselves by methods already mentioned. The whitetail makes use of a variety of food types and can survive in unusual habitats. They do require certain types and ages of plants. A vegetation type which matures and grows out of feeding whitetail's reach is of no value, and certain dried grass type plants are not used by deer because their rumen bacteria cannot metabolize them.

Fires, both controlled man-made ones and naturally-occurring burns, will improve or create new habitat. Browse type plants used by deer rapidly repopulate a burned off section of country.

Total loss of habitat in the Northern Rockies is becoming a factor to be reckoned with but as of yet is not a major problem. It remains to be seen what effect land use decisions made without deer in mind, such as dam building, road construction, urban sprawl, and logging will have.

SEMI-CONTROLLED WHITETAIL MANAGEMENT

To my knowledge, Paul Brunner is the only individual in the Northern Rockies who is making a concerted effort to manage whitetail deer in order to grow trophy animals — bucks that will score 165 to 190 Boone and Crockett points. He has had his program going now for 10 years at considerable expense and effort. His 1,560 deeded acres in westcentral Montana is bordered by leased lands. The deer are free to come and go as

"*I first got the idea to manage whitetail deer on my ranch because I'm what is known as a whitetail fanatic. Hunting is basically a big part of my life.*"— *Paul Brunner*

they please. Brunner has attempted successfully to attract and hold deer by converting his ranch into an optimum environment for them.

He has a keen sensitivity toward and understanding of whitetail deer. It shows in the numbers of trophy grade bucks he is producing. Hunting is permitted on the ranch by invitation only, and harvesting is done with archery tackle.

Brunner could be characterized as an amateur whitetail biologist who has honed his management skills through personal observations, literature study, and practical application of his acquired knowledge.

I'll let him tell his story:

"I first got the idea to manage whitetail deer on my ranch because I'm what is known as a whitetail fanatic. Hunting is basically a big part of my life. When I bought the ranch, even though it was over-grazed and run down, I knew the surrounding area was noted for holding big whitetail bucks.

"The first thing I did was have the Soil Conservation Service survey the ranch to determine what I had. The agent told me he had never seen a more abused, over-grazed ranch in his 20 years with the conservation service.

"The previous owner had run too many cattle and horses for too many years, and the vegetation had been seriously over-grazed. There was no grass, no browse, and the brushy type plants had been chewed back to twigs the size of my little finger. He had been running 125 mother cows with calves, replacement heifers, bulls, and 47 horses. The rated capacity for the ranch is something less than 50 cows.

"I hunted extensively the first winter I owned the ranch. Even though there was tracking snow during much of the season, it would be safe to say there were less than one dozen deer on the ranch. Also, I didn't see one elk track.

"After assessing the damage, the Soil Conservation Service agent and I began to formulate a plan to recover the plant communities. This plan was designed with the understanding I was more interested in raising deer and elk than cattle and horses.

"Basically, my ultimate goal was to produce good whitetail habitat and grow big bucks. We would do this in three ways: hunting would be strictly controlled, the growth of shrub-browse type plants would be encouraged in order to provide feed and cover for the deer, and finally, the numbers of domestic stock on the ranch would be strictly controlled.

"A word about controlled hunting. Initially, I had some seat-of-the-pants ideas about how best to set up a deer harvest program so as to not hurt either the deer or habitat resource but yet enhance antler size and total herd numbers. In the years since we started our ranch project, some good solid research information has been put forth — primarily from Texas game biologists.

"It is now known that not only must the habitat within which the deer live provide a good high quality type browse, but the deer herd itself must have appropriate percentages of all classes of deer. Since buck deer reach maximum body and antler development between five and six years of age, it would be wise to have a good portion of the bucks in the herd in this age group. A ratio of 50 percent of bucks above and below the five year age class would be ideal.

"How does one know the age of the bucks in a herd? Meticulous age records are kept on the harvested bucks. If the age ratios of bucks are proper it will be reflected in the kill.

"If a high percentage of bucks harvested are below the five year age class, then the number of bucks killed should be lowered. If this occurs in conjunction with too high total deer numbers in relation to the carrying capacity of the range, the number of does killed should be increased. This will accomplish two things. It will reduce the pressure on the habitat and increase the numbers of total bucks in the herd. How is this? Each doe will have twin fawns every year under optimum conditions, and on the average, one of the fawns will be a buck. By reducing habitat crowding, the remaining brood does will be healthier with higher reproductive potential and a higher fawn survival rate.

"Another indicator that does are being under-harvested is if significant numbers of does in the herd are above five years of age. The idea here is to maintain only those does with the highest reproductive capacity and most vigor. Also, if total populations of deer are high it takes more does to raise the same number of fawns on poor range than a smaller number of does could bear and raise living in prime habitat. The idea is to reduce habitat pressure by carrying fewer does but yet not suffer fewer fawns. Remember half of the fawns will be bucks.

"The ages of deer are determined by studying wear on the teeth of the lower jaw. With some study of available charts and mounted samples, it is relatively easy to very accurately determine a deer's age up to 8 1/2 years. Every deer harvested here on the ranch has its age determined. It is the best way I've found to get a feel for how the herd on the ranch is doing.

"The first problem we attacked was the over-grazing caused by the large numbers of livestock. All cattle and horses were removed from the ranch for a period of two years. I then repopulated with half a dozen mother cows and a bull. They were carefully rotated to continue encouraging the recovery of all plant species.

"During the initial two years of our recovery program we planted 105 acres of high quality hay meadow consisting primarily of alfalfa with some orchard and broom grass.

"Within the first 24 months, I began to notice a slight increase in deer numbers, but I'd have to say I didn't see a noticeable increase for five years. About the fifth year of our program, we started a very light hit and miss type feeding program only during the winter.

Strong, healthy fawns result from well nourished does.

"Our winters here are very tough but vary from year to year. An average of 18 inches of snow will lie on the ground from early December through mid-March and temperatures of 50 below zero are not uncommon. I felt there would be some benefit if we could help the deer through the winter.

"I had no scientific foundation for how or what to feed and had no idea how protein levels in feeds affected body and antler growth. As soon as I began the feeding program, which was on average about one ton per week, the numbers of deer increased dramatically, and we started for the first time seeing elk on the ranch. I noticed the elk would leave the ranch in the spring, but the deer became permanent residents.

"In the beginning I set up feed stations at trail junctions and yarding areas and fed hay which the deer were attracted to. Biologist told me deer couldn't digest hay and that in fact a steady diet of hay would kill deer. Perhaps a steady diet might have deleterious effects, but the deer flourished on a once weekly feeding schedule.

"After feeding the deer for about one year I began talking with knowledgeable whitetail hunters and read the management articles coming out of Texas. I was amazed to learn that the mineral content of a buck's diet doesn't affect antler growth nearly as much as percent and quality of dietary protein.

It has been conclusively demonstrated that the percent of protein in a buck's diet, especially early in life, plays an important role in antler development. This large forkhorn was 18 months old.

Spikes are genetically inferior animals not capable of ever growing superior antlers. They should be culled from a herd if trophy bucks are a goal of management.

"By performing carefully controlled studies, Rod Marburger, a reknowned Texas whitetail deer biologist describes in his book *King of Deer* how protein content of a deer's diet affects antler development. He took twin buck fawns and fed one an exclusive diet containing 16 percent protein. He fed the other fawn a diet of 13 percent protein. The deer were fed only these diets for one year.

"When the deer were yearlings, the buck fed 16 percent protein had antlers with four points on each side and a 16-inch spread. The deer on the low protein diet grew only one-inch-long spikes. I also learned from Marburger that bucks which were stunted early in life from being on poor range would never produce trophy racks no matter what their level of nutrition was in later life.

"Finally I learned that if a deer suffers low body weight and run-down condition because of poor habitat, his antler size will be sacrificed for the body. The body has first claim to nutrients at the expense of antler growth.

"With these ideas in mind, I began to look at different types of feeds. Presently, we are feeding seven stations on the ranch and our program is still not designed to totally support the deer. It is meant to supplement their natural foods. We religiously feed every other day using either 4-wheel-drive rigs or snowmobiles to reach the stations. We only feed during the winter. Each station gets 25 pounds of whole corn and about 25 pounds of a special high protein deer pellet I had made up specifically for deer. Plus, we put out half to one bale of high quality hay depending on how quickly the elk are eating the hay.

"This is not enough food to cause a dependency. The deer still must browse because each station has 30 to 35 deer coming to it. It does give them a good shot of fat and protein which the bucks, just coming out of rut and heading into winter, really need. Before we picked up the protein and fat content of the ration, we would invariably find winter kills around the ranch. Most of these were the bigger bucks. I have not found a single winter kill on the ranch for the past two years.

"Seven or eight years ago when we were still fumbling around with our program, we rarely saw twin fawns. Since we have upgraded our feeding routine, I haven't seen a doe with only one fawn. This is purely the result of an environment recovered enough to provide a good quality forage. Last season we saw about two to three sets of triplets. Our total permanent population of deer is probably in the neighborhood of 120 animals with an additional 60 or so that move in and out. The ratio of does to bucks among the permanent residents is about two to one.

"A very interesting piece of information I discovered while reading was bucks that grow spikes as their first set of antlers at 18 months of age are genetically inferior animals and should be culled. They, despite nutrition levels or length of life, are not capable of growing a superior set of antlers. The best they can grow is a spindly pair of forks or three points. On the

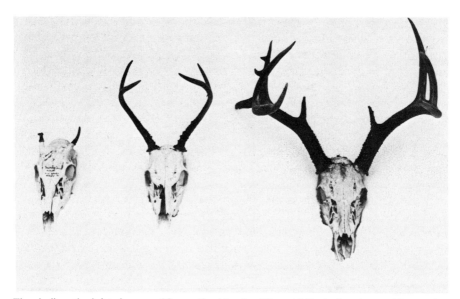

The skull on the left is from an 18-month-old spike. The middle skull is also an 18-month-old deer, while the buck on the right was 3 1/2 years old.

other hand, an 18-month-old buck that has a small basket sized three or four point rack (western count) has a good chance, given time, to produce record class antlers.

"Consequently, we attempt, and are for the most part successful, to harvest all the spikes that turn up on the ranch. We pass over the 1 1/2 to 3 1/2 year old bucks with multiple pointed racks.

"We invite certain individuals to the ranch to hunt only spikes, and they gladly do so. Our guests who want a 145 Pope and Young-points-plus buck are carefully schooled on what to shoot. The buck's rack must be heavy with long tines. The deer physically must look mature and in his prime-a blockiness to his body, heavy thick neck, and a greyish, older looking face. Older bucks will exhibit a "macho" body language. They stride with an air of dominance and confidence.

"For the last two or three years, we have really seen the quality and massiveness of the bucks' antlers improve. For example, there are four excellent trophy grade bucks that I see every day at the house feed station. We used to see lots of 18-month-old bucks that were spikes or small forkhorns, but this year we had several young bucks with nice symmetrical, slender four-point racks complete with eye guards. There is no question that if things go as they should, these better bucks will be in the Boone and Crockett class by age six.

"The largest buck taken to date off the ranch scored 180 Boone and Crockett points. Two others that were taken during the past three seasons had inside spread of 26 inches with one being a 10 by 7 and the other a 7 by 9.

"Let me summarize by touching on where we would like to take our deer program in the future. To be a good manager of whitetail deer, it is necessary to closely monitor the particular group of deer being managed and to learn everything possible about whitetail behavior. It is important not to let the deer population get ahead of the browse. Once yearly we have a wildlife biologist come in to check the condition of the range. Normally the deer browse only the buds and smaller more digestable twig tips. If the browse is chewed back to stems the size of pencils, then there is an over-population problem. This is signal to start culling deer numbers, especially does. By the way, each deer eats about six pounds of forage materials per day.

"Our main aim is to produce, every year, not one but several Boone and Crockett class bucks. I think this will be a reality in two or three more seasons which will be 12 years into our program. We want a perfect environment for breeding and to control the deer population intelligently and legally. Primarily, we would like the ranch to be a wildlife paradise on which whitetail bucks can be hunted in good whitetail habitat with the hunter experiencing as fully as possible the fair chase of a superior buck. To me it is far better for a hunter to go out and see six nice bucks but pass them over because he is looking for an older trophy grade buck rather than take the first thing with horns that moves.

"We want hunters on the ranch to be able to rattle whitetail bucks and hunt scrapes in its purest form with a minimum of disturbance to the hunters or the deer. And finally, I get a lot of personal satisfaction learning more every year about whitetail biology and observing the living, free-roaming animal."

This big-bodied, heavy-racked buck is the result of good management practices.

Author's note: I would like to comment on an idea that Rob Marburger presented in his very good text which discusses whitetail management. The idea appears in his first chapter and is so powerful I feel it needs mentioning. Rod states, "The first thing that you should burn indelibly into your brain is the fact that trophy animals no longer 'accidentally occur.' The time is gone, especially in Texas, where trophies are naturally available. Only on well managed ranges do good trophies occur." On that statement Mr. Marburger is, in my opinion, dead wrong. Good numbers of wild trophy grade and trophy class book bucks exist in huntable populations in the Northern Rockies today and for the foreseeable future. The only management practices are: controlling the number of nonresident licenses sold and limiting the number of bucks harvested by residents to one each. Collecting a trophy class whitetail buck is probably one of the greatest hunting challenges in North American today.

Now, a question-and-answer session with Paul Brunner:

Question: Paul you only allow bowhunting on the ranch. Why?

Answer: I'm not opposed to rifle hunting, having hunted with one for many years. About eight or nine years ago I took up archery and fell in love with it. Since then I have put my guns away. I despise wearing hunter orange, and I don't have to when I bowhunt. Also, rifle shots, in my opinion, disrupt the tranquility of a hunt. Most importantly, if I permitted gun hunting on the ranch the quality of the scrape and other hunting techniques we use would be compromised. Presently, we have a lot of leeway in our hunting set-ups.

Our deer are undisturbed in that they aren't exposed to the emotional trauma of gun shots. I feel because of this they maintain a more normal daily routine thus making our bowhunting strategies follow more of a pure pattern. Because of this most of our hunting is done at close range. We have a better opportunity to be very selective in harvesting just the particular buck we want to remove from the population. Gun hunters taking snap shots or long shots often misjudge the buck in the heat of the moment and may take a buck that should be left to grow a few more years.

Question: What do you think most influences antler development and size?

Answer: The most critical factor in my opinion is that the bucks come through the winter in good shape. A buck that goes into spring and is a rack of bones will put all the consumed nutrients into body recovery first, then secondly into antler growth. So a buck that enters spring in good physical condition can put more ingested protein into antler growth.

The first leafy growth in the spring has the highest protein content. As

This buck has a very unusual nontypical point arrangement on its right antler.

the vegetation matures and dries through the summer and into fall, the protein levels fall well below the optimum 16 percent level necessary for maximum antler development. If a buck's body takes until mid-July to recover muscle and fat reserves, the percent of available protein will be falling. This will adversely affect antler growth.

Genetics are also important. The bucks on our ranch seem to grow a heavier type of antlers with good tine length. The antler spread on our bucks are probably their weakest point. It is interesting that I have, on numerous occasions, been able to identify related bucks.

We are very careful to recover as many shed antlers as we can find. We find some amazing similarities in the sheds as far as tine arrangement, antler massiveness, and spread. We have found different pairs of sheds from bucks which I'm convinced are related. Two bucks which come to mind, shed both their antlers at the same feed station 36 hours apart. The antlers are very similar.

I've also found sheds in different years in the same location which I'm positive came from the same buck. The different years antlers are identical except the newer set is bigger.

Anyway, collecting and analyzing sheds is an interesting study. It gives me a good feel for how the herd and habitat on the ranch are doing.

Question: How is hunting the mountain whitetail different from its eastern cousin?

Answer: I've killed 30 or so whitetails in my home state of New Hampshire so I have a feel for the eastern deer and the type of environment they live in. The most earth-shaking difference that comes to my mind is the intensity of competition among hunters in the East. There are lots of people in the woods. Scrape hunting and rattling are of questionable value in many areas. The deer are pushed too hard.

Basic instinctive whitetail behavior is, in general the same be it in the East or West, but lack of pressure, the mountain habitat (including its remoteness and high quality forage), and the superior genetic stock in the Northern Rockies make whitetail hunting an interesting proposition.

Question: Where do you think the next world record typical whitetail buck will be taken?

Answer: There are unquestionably several such bucks in Montana. Since we have so few dedicated whitetail hunters in the state, I question whether such a buck will be harvested. They just don't get the hunting pressure. These mountain bucks are most often taken by guys hunting elk or mule deer. I personally missed a buck, because of the fever, that would have gone 210 Boone and Crockett points. This buck was in the Blackfoot Valley in western Montana.

Question: What in your opinion are the two most necessary things an archer must do to harvest a trophy grade buck?

Answer: First you have to be in an area that has the size buck you want. After that, the most important thing, technique-wise, is scouting. Scouting to me is done 12 months per year. Hiking and checking sign, driving around looking, and glassing are all important.

Next, one must figure where to set an ambush. Routes between bedding and feeding areas before the rut are good. Hunting scrapes after the rut begins are producers. Tree-standing scrapes is a favorite method of mine.

Question: At what age do you prefer to harvest bucks on the ranch?

Answer: I like to have the bucks harvested at 6 1/2 to 8 1/2 years of age when they are at their maximum development. I've got a feeling the bucks on the ranch maintain good racks into later life, so I'd prefer the bucks to be more toward the upper age range of 8 1/2 plus years of age if possible.

We routinely pass up bucks that would score 130 to 138 Pope and Young points, which is good enough to get a book listing, knowing these bucks will be much bigger if left to reach the age of 6 1/2 years or better.

Chapter Four

THE RUT AND HUNTING THEORY

The peak of the rut lasts roughly 18 to 22 days and can be a very strenuous time for the bucks, especially in a population which has a high number of mature breeding bucks. Many times I've watched bucks fussing over does for eight hours at a stretch — and the bucks never once took a bite of food even though the does were feeding in earnest.

Let me define what, in the context of this book, is meant by peak of the rut. It is the period during which a buck's behavior is modified to its greatest extent by breeding activities. During this time a hunter will have the most success taking advantage of the deer's weaknesses.

The rut can be particularly trying for bucks past their prime. It can affect their subsequent life span and social ranking. In fact, bucks in general have a shorter life span than do does.

It is important to remember that you are dealing with a different animal during the breeding cycle. The buck's behavioral characteristics change drastically — he is driven and consumed to be with does and perpetuate his species.

Rutting behavior is, to a great extent, triggered by the decreased length of day. The breeding bucks testicles begin to swell as well as his neck; both situations are caused by increasing levels of testosterone. He acquires a swollen ego too.

The doe also undergoes physiologic changes, including scent changes that take place in both her body and urine. These changes prime her prior to reaching a 24-hour period when she will ovulate during the peak of the rut when she will ovulate.

Nature times these events so there is, in the northern latitudes, a great

The doe undergoes numerous physiological changes as estrus approaches. These are recognized by the buck and he commences to rut.

crescendo of activity from approximately November 12 to November 25. Rutting intensity, not timing, can be modified by weather. A cold snap or a severe snowstorm followed by clear, cold weather will tend to spur on the festivities.

In a well-balanced herd, bucks up to 2 1/2 years of age may have no opportunity to exhibit a rutting attitude. They may show no physical or emotional evidence of being rutty. The mature breeding bucks so suppress them that they are completely cowed. In an imbalanced herd, the younger bucks must and do play a vital role in impregnating the does. There are not enough larger, older bucks around to get the job done.

Older breeding bucks will be loners at this time and will not tolerate the presence of another mature buck, although they may tolerate a very young subordinate one. During the summer the social order and dominance among the bachelor male groups is established. The bucks in a given range know each other very well by the onset of the rut, with the older bucks already having established themselves high in the pecking order.

This is where antlers come in. They are not defensive weapons in the strictest sense of the term as fights among bucks are very rare, occurring only if two bucks are very nearly equal in body size and antler mass. Antlers in reality reflect the vigor and health of the buck and serve as visual indicators of such to their peers and to the does. A buck with a large, heavy rack will be near the top of the social scale.

There are two types of visual signposts that a breeding buck creates before and during the rutting period. These are the scrape and the rub, both of which must be thoroughly understood if the hunter is to plan a hunt with some purpose — especially if one is seeking a special buck.

Let me qualify the suggestion of "thoroughly understood" by adding that by saying "understood to the present degree of our knowledge as presented by biologists, researchers, and expert whitetail hunters."

First, it is a misconception to believe that bucks stake out and defend a territory. They are not territorial and will not defend a specific piece of ground marked by rubs and scrapes. The buck's wandering ranges will often overlap as they follow the does in estrus. During the rut, a buck's range may expand to encompass 10 to 12 square miles.

Nor are whitetail bucks polygamous. They do not gather harems of does as a bull elk herds his cows. Mule deer bucks will fall somewhere in between, keeping watch over a loose-knit band of does moving in or out of an area.

Scrapes begin to appear a week to 10 days before the rut nears its peak. Their size and numbers increase as rutting activity intensifies. Their appearance signifies things are beginning to heat up. Numerous scrapes are placed throughout a buck's home range. The buck will paw the ground with a front foot and scatter the leaves and duff, exposing bare soil. Scrapes vary considerably in size with 24 by 18 inches about average. They are frequently located on a trail, be it an old logging road or deer trail, etc., or in a small clearing.

A buck may mark his scrapes with urine and/or his preorbital scent glands. Very frequently after making a scrape, he stands over it and will urinate or rub-urinate into it. He may then also grasp a twig or branch over the scrape in his mouth and release it, letting it spring back over his preorbital scent gland. Very often a single track will be left in the soft earth of the scrape as the buck walks off, though the footprint probably was not left intentionally. What the buck is in effect doing is setting out advertising posts to does approaching estrus. There is recent evidence that scrapes may also serve as "threat" displays to other bucks. Bucks have been observed making a scrape in the presence of a subordinate buck.

The terms primary and secondary scrapes have been bantered about. What do they mean? A buck does not make a primary scrape per se, but starts out as previously described with a series of small, scent-marked scrapes throughout his home range. Scrape patterns can be further confused by numerous small scrapes being made by adolescent bucks following their instincts. A doe, in estrus and attracted by the urine odor of a scrape, will cross-urinate the scrape site and wander off. She has now in effect created a primary scrape which can and will be checked by more than one buck.

In reality, all breeding bucks in the area tend to converge on a so called primary scrape. The scrape site will look more active. It may be larger with pawed dirt scattered in all directions. There will not be a thin layer of leaves or pine needles beginning to cover the soil as will accumulate in a neglected secondary scrape. Fresh, urine-soaked earth may be present and finally the scrape may have a pronounced odor. Sometimes these primary scrapes can be used season after season by succeeding generations of deer.

A breeding buck wanders through its home range, checking his marked scrapes. He may or may not check it with his physical presence but perhaps scent check it from heavy cover located downwind. If he finds it cross-urinated by a receptive doe, he will immediately begin to track her.

He does this in a very deliberate fashion with nose hard to the ground, resembling a hound trailing a rabbit. Bucks appear to be especially vulnerable at this stage. On numerous occasions I have seen them so intent on a doe's scent trail that the buck literally walked within a few feet of me. Several have actually paused and looked directly at me and, seemed to care less, and then put their nose back to the ground and trotted off.

After catching the doe, a buck will assume a courtship posture. His neck is extended and lowered with his chin slightly elevated. He frequently emits a low, raspy bleating sound much like a squeaky, quickly opened door with a rusty hinge. It is clearly audible several yards away. The doe frequently urinates at this point to keep the buck informed as to her ovulating status. The buck continually follows her anywhere she goes, a few paces behind.

To be honest, until four years ago I was unaware bucks made a soft, bleating call to the does. While photographing mule deer one November, I saw a buck in courting posture call to a doe he was trailing. Three seasons later I was able to take a whitetail buck because I was able to recognize the sound.

The weather was bitter that particular December, and I had climbed into my tree-stand with about 40 minutes of shooting light left. At minus 5 degrees Fahrenheit, that is about all the time I could take standing in a tree.

The rub is an important signpost that the rut has begun and a breeding buck is in the area. Look for concentrations of rubs when four to six can be viewed while standing in one place.

Right at dark three does filtered through the brush to the trail where my tree-stand was placed. They filed nicely by a few yards below my feet. In the failing light, I scanned the brush along the does' backtrail and saw a shadowy form paralleling the deer run. The deer came abreast of my stand at 15 yards and stopped. I had a narrow shooting lane right to its chest, even though the brush was so thick I couldn't see the deer's head. I had a hunch it was a buck as it was alone, showing interest in the does, and hanging in the brush. Something had to give quickly as the light was fading.

It did. The deer made a fatal mistake. He grunted softly to the departing does. I knew instantly it was a buck. Anchoring my arrow, I drove it nicely through his lungs.

Fighting occurs among dominant bucks immediately prior to and for several hours after copulation. The tending buck will defend the doe from other bucks for as long as 24 hours after breeding. He is not defending a specific piece of ground but his right to the doe. He may mate several times with the doe during this 24-hour period.

Therein lies the logic of rattling antlers as a hunting technique. If a buck hears two others fighting he may come in, assuming there is a doe in estrus present. (More on rattling later.)

The second important signpost of the rut is the rub. Suffice it to say, bucks begin rubbing trees as soon as their antlers are hard, beginning in early September. This timing coincides with the shedding of velvet. The drying and shedding of antler velvet is linked to rising testosterone levels. The velvet can dry, crack, and fall off with or without rubbing. Increased rubbing activity is also linked to rising testosterone levels. It is notable that wild bucks with testicular damage or undescended testicles will never shed their antler velvet covering.

In the Northern Rockies, rubbing starts in early September, and the bucks rub until the antlers are shed. Trees selected most often are four to five inches in diameter and apparently there is no correlation as to the size of the rubbed tree to the size of the buck. A buck simply rubs what is available in his home range.

As a buck moves through his home range, he will make rubs along his everyday travel routes. Careful observation will show these rubs sometimes occur in a line and may parallel a buck's main travel routes. Rubs are one more visible piece of evidence showing how a buck moves through his home range.

It is important to age a rub to predict current activity in a buck's home range. The peeled bark at the margins of a recent rub will appear clean and supple. The exposed wood will be white and feel damp. Fresh, gooey sap may be present. Older September and early October rubs will show dried brown, brittle bark and the exposed wood will be a dry and brown-grey in color. More significance can be applied to fresh rubs made in November than those made in September. They simply indicate more up-

Undisturbed rutting behavior is best demonstrated where the mature buck to doe ratio is high and the deer aren't overly disturbed.

to-date information on a buck's movements.

There appear to be two reasons breeding bucks make rubs. First, they serve to mark his regular travel routes. Rubs will be more numerous and clustered in his core area, especially closer to bedding areas. Second, rubs serve as communication between sexes. It is common for a buck to rub its forehead gland on a rub tree, imprinting his individualistic scent on it. Other deer of both sexes will sniff and lick these forehead and antler rubbed trees.

It should be noted here that the forementioned situations, causes, and effects occur under ideal conditions. The importance a hunter can place on rubs and scrapes depends directly on the social importance they serve for the particular herd being hunted. The creation of rubs and scrapes and their use by the local deer population depends on habitat type, weather, density, age, and sex ratio of the deer.

Typically, many whitetail herds in the United States have a high percentage of does. Most of the bucks in these herds are under 3 1/2 years of age and don't have trophy racks. This will nullify or greatly reduce the social function and communicative role of rubs and scrapes. In your hunting situation, there may be no scraping activity at all, especially if the terrain is open. In open country deer rely more on visual clues expressed by body language than on sign post communication.

To have successful rub and scrape hunting, many factors must come together simultaneously along with a good dose of luck. It is naive to expect to locate a rub or scrape, throw up a tree-stand, and then simply collect the boss buck of the woods.

In the Northern Rockies, there is intense scraping and rubbing activity because of a thickly-wooded country and a high number of big breeding bucks and mature does. The buck-doe ratio is also good throughout most of the whitetails' range. It is really quite fun to hunt whitetails when they are demonstrating their repetiteur of rutting behavior. If conditions are "just right", including the buck's mental attitude, old mossyhorn will act like he read the book and follow a predictable pattern right to your meat pole. It kind of reminds me of hunting bull elk. When they're hot, a bull elk will bugle back at just about any sound, including the opening of a creaky pickup truck door. Again, the function of rubbing and scraping is not fully understood. For example, it has been recently demonstrated that does on occasion also make scrapes and will do so in any season of the year.

If a trophy grade buck, one scoring 145 to 160 Boone and Crockett points, has an Achille's heel, it is during the peak of the rut. Fortunately the Northern Rockies deer season meshes perfectly with the timing of the rut.

The breeding bucks tend to be less cautious, more active during the daylight hours, and most importantly can be found away from heavy cover.

All these factors are related to the estrus stage of the does and how sexually active a buck is at a given point of time. What I'm saying is that if a doe is particularly sensuous and triggers a buck that is primed, even though he may by nature be reclusive, as all trophy-age animals are, he might make a fatal error! The trick is to place oneself in a position to take advantage of the buck's mistake. This will be discussed in depth in a later chapter.

In my opinion, there are certain record-class bucks that will score over 170 Boone and Crockett points that never show themselves for any reason, doe or no doe. They are hyper-cautious and super-reclusive. And I suppose, after all, that is why each of us keeps the fire in our gut burning. Maybe one cold November day we'll catch him in a compromised situation.

Although his rack is small and in the velvet, this buck already has big bases and a heavy brow tine.

The whitetail habitat of northern Idaho and western Montana is heavily timbered and rugged.

Chapter Five

HUNTING THE ROCKY MOUNTAIN WHITETAIL

In 1982, approximately 3,000,000 whitetail deer were harvested by 12,000,000 hunters in the United States and Canada — about a 25 percent success rate. In Idaho there were 8,000 whitetail deer harvested while in Montana hunters bagged 27,456 whitetails.

Hunting whitetail deer in the Northern Rockies can in some localities be difficult. In Montana's Swan Valley, bagging a whitetail is enjoyed by about 17 to 24 percent of the hunters annually. The environment along the Swan Range is densely timbered with an understory of heavy alder brush in many areas. Seeing deer and getting a clear shot can be difficult but worth the effort as this area is a prime spot. Other areas like the Bitterroot Valley in western Montana offer a more open type habitat, and hunter success is much higher.

Many of us will never have the opportunity to hunt British Columbia, Alaska, or any of the other glamour spots — schedules or economic restraints make that an impossible dream. To most of us, the whitetail deer is our Dall sheep, mountain goat, and Alaska-Yukon moose all wrapped into one. The whitetail deer is the common man's trophy, and a fine one it is! It can be hunted on your own, close to home in an evening after work, with a little homework. Hunting in the Northern Rockies gives one a chance to hunt big whitetail bucks in a beautiful environment.

Much of what is published and spoken as gospel about deer hunting methods is only speculation. Bold statements are made based on the happenings during one or two hunts. Further, some of what appears in national hunting publications is gobbledegook which either doesn't apply, is impractical, or has been printed so many times it is sickening.

Because whitetail deer are so popular and so widely hunted, there have been more hunting theories, styles, and techniques presented discussing whitetail hunting than just about any other outdoor subject. Almost everyone who has hunted more than two seasons or killed a whitetail has firm convictions about how it should be done. Whitetail hunters live in nearly every geographic location in the United States and come from all sorts of economic, ethnic, and social backgrounds. It's no wonder there is a wide diversity of opinion concerning the whitetail.

What follows is a description of hunting techniques best suited to the Northern Rockies, but which applies to many other areas of the country also. They are not gut feelings or hocus pocus. I have visited on numerous occasions with the most knowledgeable whitetail hunters in these mountains and picked their brains. Many are students of the whitetail every day, all year long. They, as the old cliche goes, eat, drink, and sleep whitetail deer 24 hours a day either in the woods scouting, sitting in a tree-stand observing, or talking about deer with other hunters.

I've looked for common denominators. What do I hear, see, and discuss with individuals that occurs over and over? What ideas and observations keep popping up over and over again? These ideas, after a time, come to be accepted as fact. This is what this chapter will relay to you as learned from the giants in whitetail circles. I will intermingle my thoughts and experiences with theirs. I will be satisfied if I can cause you to retain a few pertinent facts about hunting mountain whitetails. Therefore I will limit our discussions to hunting methods most productive and/or popular in this region of the country. They are: tree-stand hunting, still hunting, and antler rattling. These techniques however, apply in many instances to whitetail hunting anywhere.

Thinking back again to the idea of living whitetails 24 hours a day, I'm reminded of an analogy. I'm considered to be a fairly decent wildlife photographer. I'm often asked at various seminars how I take all those close pictures of animals. I credit it to persistence; no hurdle is too big, no time taken too long. Achieving a set goal is the most important factor.

I've seen so-called "dedicated wildlife photographers" run up to a bull elk, shoot 10 or 12 pictures and consider it a good day and leave. I consider this akin to sitting in my living room watching a man walk down the sidewalk as he passes in and out of the limited view of a window. I can observe him maybe one minute, certainly not enough time to learn what his name is, where he lives, or the size and color of his shoes.

When I get on a bull elk in the morning, I feed with him, bed with him, wallow with him, and in short stay on the bull until last light. As the day unfolds, the bull slowly reveals what he is, where he sleeps, and how he peels off a lodgepole pine with his antlers. He has graciously given me a look into his private life because I had the interest, patience, and dedication to take the time to do so. I may take 150 pictures over the course of the experience. Now that is high adventure!

Hunting whitetail from tree-stands is a very effective way to neutralize the deer's sense of smell and hearing. Proper placement of the stand is critical.

Anyway, to be a successful whitetail hunter who consistently (every other season or so) takes trophy grade bucks, we have to think in such terms. Going out three or four days a year with no scouting and no understanding of the species is usually a waste of time. Of course, as stated before, when hunting we must select an area that has big bucks in it. There are certain areas that produce big bucks year after year either because of high quality forage, the deer are older, lack of hunting pressure, or any combination thereof.

Oftentimes an area that produces big bucks won't produce them for long because word gets out. Personally, I don't foresee this problem in the future in the Northern Rockies. The country is rugged and discourages many hunters while offering superb seclusion for the bucks.

The so-called glamour species such as elk, mule deer, bear, and cougar come to mind when people start talking about hunting Montana and Idaho. Whitetail deer will probably continue to be the neglected big game species of the Northern Rockies. This is precisely the kind of neglect big bucks need to grow old.

In addition, the bucks are spread over a tremendous expanse of country and not concentrated in any one area, prohibiting their exploitation in any one locality.

How does a mountain whitetail mesh with its environment? Basically it has the same outlook on life and species characteristics of its brothers in any other part of the country. Its entire world is influenced by its belly, the rut, and security needs. One other vital influence of its life in the mountains is the weather. It is sure to weed out the inferior animals and influence the deer's behavior a great deal during all seasons.

It helps, too, if we put ourselves inside a whitetail's skin. They are a prey animal with an innate awareness. Their kind have been devoured by a variety of predators for thousands of years. They are in a constant state of anxiety, ever alert. In their mind, every bush and rock hides potential danger.

The next time you see a wild deer, watch its ears, eyes, and nose. They are constantly tuned to the deer's surroundings. Deer cannot think or reason, but their computer-like brain is programmed at birth to instinctively react in predetermined ways to a given situation. The trophy grade bucks have gone beyond instinctive behavior. They are the chosen few which learn by cause and effect to avoid certain situations. Maybe "learn" is too strong a word, but they certainly have a memory honed by cause and effect situations. Boone and Crockett class bucks are enigmatic, reclusive, and elusive to say the least.

As for hunting technique, I'm not going to tell you the following methods are golden. They are however, based on sound principles gained for the most part from reading, discussions with other hunters whose opinions are respected, and a lot of hours spent in the woods watching and studying deer — and not just during hunting season.

The ideas are meant to supplement your present knowledge and to be used or disregarded as you see fit. Many situations apply to whitetail hunting anywhere but emphasis, as noted previously, will be on procedures and techniques that work most satisfactorily in the Northern Rockies.

STAND HUNTING

Since most of us cannot help being affected by the hustle and bustle rat race we all run every day, sitting still in a tree for any length of time can be almost impossible. It seems unnatural to sit still in a serene setting for a prolonged period of time. Some of the very best deer and elk hunters I'm acquainted with absolutely can't sit still on the ground or in a tree and refuse to even entertain the idea.

For some reason (I suspect it is some sort of acquired mental deficiency) I have been blessed with the ability to tolerate considerable periods of time perched in a tree. From before first light to after last light is no problem, and, in fact, I have been known to sleep overnight in a tree-stand in order to blend in a little more with the rhythm of the woods. When I was a kid I had a kind of perverted fantasy in which I would construct and then stay in a tree house high in a cypress tree overlooking a section of swamp for about a month just to see what forms of life passed underneath. By the way, I never did fulfill the fantasy!

At any rate, a person can train and discipline himself to sit the required amount of time in a stand. I don't hesitate to say tree-stand hunting is the most consistently successful method used to take whitetail deer.

Most of the battle is psychological. You must believe that tree sitting will work and stick with it long enough to let it succeed. Placement of the stand must be such that you firmly believe there are deer in the area and in fact your stand is placed such that deer will pass close enough to it to afford a shot. Once you believe this then it is easier to beat the impatience factor.

I would tell you to take reading materials into a stand, which I have done a time or two but, sure enough, the second you look to a page, Mr. Big steps out and catches you. It is important to continually work your head and eyes searching the ground cover, and it takes discipline. Deer will appear before your eyes as if by magic —nothing one second, and "poof" there he is. You heard or sensed nothing. It's like magic.

I realize that staying attentive continually for six to eight hours is impossible. I would suggest staying very alert the first three hours of daylight and during the last two hours before dark. During these times, it is a good idea to stand. This will put you in a better position to shoot and by rotating your head slowly, a better view of the ground can be had. If an all-day stay in the stand is planned, it is best to relax during the midday stretch. Actually, the daylight hours in the Northern Rockies are brief during November. Shooting light is about 7·45 a.m. and ends at 4:55 p.m. give

Staying alert and being patient can pay big dividends while tree-stand hunting. Gene Wensel in action.

or take a few minutes, depending on a clear or overcast day.

Seeing the deer first, as he moves into range, is very helpful. Then there is time to carefully change positions for a better shot if necessary and to prepare your weapon to shoot. It is an excellent idea to spend the first few minutes after entering a stand to raising your gun or bow to an imagined shooting posture and work out any kinks in your shooting motion. The moment of truth, when it comes, won't allow for any wasted motions or miscalculations. Deer do look up.

For example, I was in a stand of cypress trees bordering Reedy Creek in central Florida. The area is a dense swamp and holds good populations of deer. I was a freshman hunter at the time but was smart enough to place my tree-stand on a trail that a single animal was using to exit the swamp cover to go to his feeding area in a large, brushy savannah. As I recall, it was a very cold morning for Florida — the temperature being around 34 degrees. Consequently, I was wearing a fairly heavy coat.

I was in my stand before first light and stood leaning against the tree trunk with my iron sighted 30-30 at ready. I placed the muzzle end of the rifle against the boards of the stand next to my right foot and held the butt plate in my right hand so I could raise the gun to firing position with a minimum of motion.

Dawn came and went and the sun was beginning to warm things up a bit. Various birds, falling pine cones, and scurrying squirrels kept my head swiveling like a puppet's all morning. The swamp floor was covered with all sorts of crackling debris and I felt there was a good chance of hearing the deer before seeing it, so I checked every little noise.

About 9:00 a.m. I was thinking about abandoning my project when I heard the snap of the 10,000th twig that morning. Easing my head to the left, I saw a whitetail buck. He was the first buck I ever had the opportunity to take. The buck was tiptoeing through the cypress trunks about 30 yards from my stand, heading toward the edge of the swamp. (Why he was heading away from his bedding area into his feeding area at that time of day I'll never know.)

Needless to say, my heart was about to pop out of my chest as I began to slowly raise my 30-30. The buck was very methodically moving past the left side of my stand. As my rifle came up, the hammer caught in the fabric under the waist flap of my coat. I glanced down at the coat as I attempted pulling harder to release the rifle — but no luck. Looking back to the buck, I saw he had put several cypress trees between me and him, and he was still walking.

I tugged and fiddled with the rifle hammer and coat and began to get a creeping sense of panic. I couldn't believe this beautiful trophy was going to walk away. Looking down again to the coat, I gave it my full attention and finally untangled it from the rifle's hammer.

I brought the gun to my shoulder as my eyes sought the buck. He happened just then to stop and pause, with his chest clearly exposed, between two trees about 50 yards out. I squeezed the trigger just like in practice. He fell over like he had been struck by lightning.

I was so carried away with the event that I forgot where I was and jumped the 10 feet to the ground. Let me tell you, a wet peat bog is no place to jump into. I went down to my waist in muck and couldn't claim my trophy for another few minutes.

This short hunting tale illustrates the importance of testing your set-up prior to settling into serious standing. Creaking boards, rattling chains, bulky clothing, or any variety of circumstances can cause a missed opportunity.

Why are tree-stands so effective? For one thing, whitetail deer are predictable if not pressured too bad. They have the same daily routines, using the same bedding and feeding areas and travel lanes. Therefore a stand can be set up, after studying the situation, and the deer can be caught making his rounds. It is the only way to hunt whitetails and somewhat neutralize their acute senses of hearing, smell, and sight. If those three factors can be negated or controlled, it gives the hunter a tremendous advantage.

The use of a tree-stand will very effectively take away 100 percent of a deer's hearing. Board platforms or portable stands should be built and placed solidly so there is no creaking or rattling as one shifts his weight. Snow and ice should be cleaned off upon entering the stand.

An elevated stand will take away a deer's eyes about nine out of 10 times. Deer, their peripheral vision being what it is and if they have had experience with tree-stand hunters, will be more likely to see movement and look up. Even then, all is not necessarily lost. Very often a hunter can escape detection by remaining absolutely motionless. The deer, not conditioned to expect danger from above, may lose interest and move off or relax.

The deer's nose is the most difficult problem to contend with while tree-stand hunting. Tree-stands are effective methods by which a deer's sense of smell can be fooled. But, if a deer comes in downwind, there is a fair chance he will catch the human scent. A slight, steady breeze blowing away from the deer's expected approach route is best.

Finally, a tree-stand affords a good view. Being above the brush level gives the sportsman a terrific advantage. A good line of sight can be had for 360 degrees and extending out some distance, depending on the ground cover. A stand height of 10 to 15 feet is good, but I've had success using stands as low as 8 feet.

Personally, it gives me a psychological advantage to know I've got a good chance to see the deer first. I can then prepare myself to shoot before the deer actually is in range. As mentioned earlier, sometimes the deer are suddenly there, materializing out of thin air. Now the equation is complicated because the correct moment must be chosen to risk moving a weapon into shooting position.

View from a tree-stand. Remember to aim arrow or bullet slightly low on the target area. This buck should be left to grow to his potential.

A gun or bow is readied in super slow motion only when the deer's head is turned behind a tree or as the deer begins to move away from the stand. If not, he will likely detect any quick motion and catch the hunter with his weapon half ready. Once detected, there is a staring and waiting contest. This plays into the deer's hand, so to speak, as he spends his entire life patiently tring to figure out any unusual situations in his environment. It never ceases to amaze me how long a deer can stand rock-still and stare. By sheer perservance, they frequently force the composure of the hunter to yield and thereby win the contest.

Placement of the tree-stand is, of course, the most critical factor. If a stand is in the wrong place, no amount of sitting will produce a thing. Here is where scouting comes into play.

The key word when discussing scouting is to be observant. Don't walk through the woods thinking about how you're going to make next month's mortgage payment. I used to think scouting was necessary only a few days before the season began and actually did much of my scouting while hunting. This approach especially hinders the chances of bagging a trophy grade buck as they require more time to figure out. Attempt to scout as often as possible throughout the year. The puzzle pieces will fall together more quickly.

In order to successfully scout an area, it is important to know how to read sign and understand what you see. This can only come from doing a lot of legwork in the area to be hunted and seeing a lot of sign — in other words, time and experience. Reading what other knowledgable hunters have to say about sign interpretation will help round out your thoughts.

When scouting with the thought of placing a tree-stand, be discreet, brief, and low key. I try to scout alone; one person, no talking, and with only two feet moving through the deer's home range. I try to locate where the sign is freshest and thickest. Where are the deer most of the time? Observe rubs, scrapes, trails, tracks, bedding areas, and feeding spots. In other words, I'm trying to get a picture of what the deer are doing and where they are moving.

Now all this information tends to become muddled and confused, especially if you're like me — over 40 years old. So take a legal pad and draw a picture of the area and where in the area the sign is located. After two or three trips into a prospective hunting spot, a pattern will begin to develop. You may be able to piece together movement tendencies. If travel lanes between bedding and feeding areas can be established, you are in good shape. Or maybe an active primary scrape can be found which is another excellent stand sight.

I'd like to mention a scouting technique Gene Wensel discusses in his book *Hunting Rutting Whitetails*. That is backtracking deer to see where they have been and what they have been doing. It is a method I'd never thought of using but it makes good sense. It's obvious that some good, sound information can be obtained this way. One of Gene's favorite times to scout is December and January after the regular season is over. He lays the groundwork for the next season.

Once the scouting information is as complete as possible, a stand sight can be selected.

Before the rut commences, the best chance of taking a trophy grade buck would be to place a stand over its feeding routes. Big bucks are very nocturnal except, and sometimes even, during the rut. So the first few minutes and the last few minutes of shooting light are the most productive. And I mean few minutes. All your senses should be working hard in the fading light of evening or the dim pre-dawn grey. Deer appear as ghostly shadows and can be difficult to see. Relying on your ears to tune in on a snapped twig may make the difference. A few precious seconds of evening light may be salvaged by placing a stand closer to the bedding area. By the time a buck has ambled its way to its feeding sight, it is often dark. In a similar vein, it may leave its night feeding area before shooting light and head for its bed. Therefore, more shooting light will be available the closer it gets to its bed. Considering these types of movement patterns sometimes will provide the necessary edge to take the buck of your dreams.

One more thing I go to a great deal of effort for is to locate some sort of a bottleneck along the deer's trail as close as possible to my selected stand site. I'm looking for some natural occurring obstacle or topographical feature that will funnel a buck through a certain point on the trail. If luck permits there will be an appropriate stand tree near this bottleneck. I can now predict exactly where the deer will travel and how far away it will be. A particularly thick patch of brush and trees through which its trail passes or a point at which a well-worn trail funnels to and crosses a creek would be such spots. This bottleneck ideally should have low hanging branches or blowdown timber in it which may in fact be part of the bottleneck itself. As the deer approaches these obstacles, its attention will momentarily be on ducking its head through or stepping over these natural barriers. At this precise moment, the hunter will have an opportunity to raise his bow or rifle and remain undetected while making his shot.

Scrape hunting is a different story. During the rut, normal feeding patterns are altered. Bucks feed very little during that period. Scrape hunting presents an opportunity to harvest a specific buck which may well be the dominant buck of the area. Hot, primary scrapes probably only have a life span of 14 to 18 days so it is important to be on top of the situation and stay current on the area's activities.

Naturally, the problem is finding which scrape to watch. Hopefully, through scouting, you already have a good feel for the most active areas in a buck's home range and have an idea where to start looking for an active primary scrape. If a primary scrape can be located on a trail along the buck's line of travel, his movements can be plotted more accurately. Remember, the primary scrape sight is a hub of activity and the area should be entered and exited quietly and quickly. A stand can be placed either overlooking the scrape or downwind 30 or 40 yards to catch the buck, hopefully between your stand and the scrape when he scent-checks the scrape.

It may be possible, and indeed may be a good idea, to try to tailor a hunt to fit a certain situation, terrain type, or any unusual circumstances. The buck may be scent-checking a scrape, he may be more active during the day than night, or he may be more vulnerable on a travel route between two scrapes. Again experience will give you a feel for selecting the correct ambush sight, time and place.

Much has been written about methods of approach and getting into stands. Granted, caution should be exercised — no excessive noise such as coughing or clanging on the steps of the stand. The wind should not blow human scent toward and across the scrape or toward bedding areas.

However, in my opinion, there are certain situations and types of habitat in which caution to the point of rubber gloves and scent soaked boots are going too far. An urbanized buck like the one I told you about, living next to my home, will take little notice of a few molecules of human scent on the forest floor. He deals with it all the time. But a totally wild buck will retire quickly or at least become more reclusive and cautious at the slightest hint of a human in the area. Lots of times I've had deer walk directly across the scent trail which I made while getting into my stand and not give a second look.

When considering the above paragraph, keep in mind that trophy-grade bucks and bigger, urbanized or not, will be more protective of their hides.

I must share one final thought with you about stand hunting. Some of my most vivid and pleasurable outdoor adventures have occurred while stand sitting. After a few minutes, I begin to feel like part of the environment — kind of blend in, so to speak. I feel privileged to watch the happenings of the forest creatures as they go about their daily lives.

I once saw an ermine chase a red squirrel in and out of a pile of blow-down. The squirrel, screaming in terror, managed to escape to his nest hole. Oftentimes, chickadees perch on my bow limb. I once had a bobcat steal past the base of my tree. These looks into nature's intimacies are precious to me and add a lot to my life.

On another subject, I've solved a lot of personal problems, formulated game plans for financial dealings, and in general put my emotional house in order during the slack periods of woods watching. I feel mentally organized and ready to attack the rat race after a good long session in a tree.

STILL-HUNTING

Still-hunting is hunting in its purist form. I'm a reasonably proficient still-hunter and enjoy the technique, but I would say there are very few people who are expert at it. I work hard at it every season trying to improve. Done properly, still-hunting takes extreme discipline, self control, and mental skills to interpret what is going on in the environment around us. I would also say that taking a deer this way is a very rewarding experience. In a way, it is beating a deer at its own game in its own surroundings. Whitetail deer are probably the most difficult big game species in the world to still-hunt.

I believe there are certain types of terrain, and certain weather conditions in which it is impossible to still-hunt effectively. Good timing, being in the right place at the right time, is important too. Expert still-hunters seem to have sense for making good things happen.

Here's my assessment of what still-hunting is. It is a method of hunting in which the hunter attempts to move through an area as quietly and unobtrusively as possible while maintaining a razor's edge of alertness in

Still hunting whitetail deer is hunting in its most demanding and satisfying form. This form of hunting takes on a deer on its own terms. Seeing the buck first is the key.

order to spot game before he himself is detected.

It is a game of supreme skills learned only after many hours and seasons of practice. Not everyone can learn it. The accomplished still-hunter will suffer many frustrations practicing his trade, and these failures must be accepted as a learning experience.

Still-hunting is a solo sport, and in a way still-hunting well is an expression of an individual's personality and appreciation of a total outdoor experience. A confirmed still-hunter wants freedom from hearing another human voice or foot fall. He wants nothing to break his bond with the environment and the game sought, be it only for a few hours. He, because of his soloist activities, will cause the least disturbance to the deer population.

A definition of what a still-hunter isn't is a person who wanders at random through the woods, without a feel for the natural world around him, hoping to get a snap shot at a white flag.

To put still-hunting in its proper perspective, think of it this way. The hunter pits his ears and nose against those of a whitetail buck, and of course it is no contest. Humans are simply outmatched. A mature, older buck makes the problem more difficult. But we do have two superior weapons — our eyes and brains which, if used properly, can increase the odds of collecting a buck. To successfully still-hunt we must use our eyes to see the sign and read the lay of the land. Our brain will then interpret and act on what we see. Lots of fast leg work has no place in still-hunting.

Upon entering the woods and beginning a hunt, it is imperative that we shed the burden that society places on each of us. Just like a layer of clothing, we must strip our mind of kids, appointments, and next week's tasks. This is the most difficult part of still-hunting for me. I find it hard to clear my mental processes and get what I call into-the-rhythm of a hunt. If that isn't possible on a given day, it's probably best to give it up or climb into your favorite tree-stand where mental lapses are more forgivable.

The deer we hope to harvest, on the other hand, doesn't suffer that problem — ever. Let's picture him in our minds. Time means absolutely nothing. He has no appointments and no place he must be. He has no sense of urgency. He is in perfect rhythm with his environment at all times, rarely letting his guard down. His mind isn't cluttered with useless nonsense.

To illustrate some of the finer points of still-hunting, let me take you through a hunt I experienced last season.

The ridge I was hunting came up out of a narrow, rocky, heavily-timbered canyon and climbed sharply. As the ridge gained altitude, it held semi-flat, lightly timbered benches every so often. It was in one of these small openings that I hoped to catch a buck. The crown of the ridge was narrow and covered with beargrass, light brush, and medium to large diameter pine trees. The trees under the ridge were lodgepole pine, branchless to a height of about 25 feet. The flanks of the ridge were heavily timbered and fell off sharply. I had scouted the area on numerous occasions and had a good feel for buck movement patterns. It was during the rut, and I knew the bucks would be moving down and across the ridge to check the does. Because I knew the area so well, I wouldn't be breaking my concentration by looking down for sign. I knew the deer were there.

Being intimately familiar with the terrain hunted will tip the scales of success greatly in your favor. This lessens the mental power used worrying about where you are. Most importantly, the location of likely hot spots and "bucky" areas is known ahead of time, allowing compensation for wind direction. As these areas are approached, progress can be slowed to below a snail's pace.

Some types of terrain don't fit well into still-hunting procedures. Very open country offers no concealment for the hunter, while country choked with brush and or blow-down may be too difficult to move through quietly while remaining alert.

One must have faith in his chosen area. Mental intensity is directly proportional to belief that deer are ahead, that it is possible to see a keeper buck at any moment. Any portion of an area that you feel holds no deer should be moved through quickly. It is trying enough to maintain mental alertness in an area where deer are known to be, let alone a questionable area. This faith in the area hunted will keep you going.

The weather this particular morning was perfect. In the pre-dawn darkness, I rode my horse three miles into the canyon. There was light rain but no wind. The woods were soggy and quiet with low-hanging cloud banks. There was no snow on the ground and the temperature hovered at 40 degrees.

Weather conditions being as fickle as they are in the Northern Rockies, clothing selection is an important consideration when still-hunting. Some heavy climbing may precede long periods of relative inactivity causing fluctuations in body temperatures. Therefore it is a good idea to wear clothing in layers.

From the inside out, I wear a T-shirt, long underwear, light wool long-sleeved shirt, and down vest with the whole works covered by a heavy wool jacket topped with a thin blaze orange covering. Wool pants, wool felt-lined rubber-bottomed leather upper boots, a wool stocking hat, and wool gloves complete the outfit.

As the day warms or I'm doing some heat-producing climbing, the layers are stripped off and placed in or on a day pack until the desired body temperature is reached. Wool gives two advantages. It is a very quiet fabric much like the hair of a deer, and it will maintain body heat even if wet. In the negative column, wool does become heavy when it's wet.

During archery season, light wool or cotton clothing earth-tone in color and possibly covered with camo coveralls of a soft cotton material is a good bet.

Weather affects still hunting in two ways. It helps hide our human clumsiness or amplifies it. Second, it affects the mood of the deer.

During a light rain or a damp, foggy, windless day, footfalls and movements are muffled and deer seem, for some reason, to be complacent and less attentive. Occasionally they even seem to be lethargic.

Soft, damp snow of 2 to 4 inches in depth also muffles sound, provides better vision of the game, and provides tracking snow in the event an animal isn't killed outright. Tracking deer while hunting in snow has been unproductive for me. Invariably, I jump the deer while I'm studying the direction of the track. Once I cut a fresh trail I still hunt through the area paying no attention to the track. I just assume the deer is close by. Also, it is impossible to accurately and consistently determine the size of the buck being followed by looking at his track. Hunting time is too valuable to waste it following a big-footed doe or younger buck.

There are certain days that weather conditions prohibit still-hunting with any degree of success. Prolonged dry spells, crusty snow, strong winds all make conditions difficult. Still-hunting can still be successful under these conditions but much greater periods of time must be spent standing still and watching. When conditions are dry or snow crusted our feeble human ears become more valuable. On many occasions by having patience and being quiet, I've been able to hear and subsequently see deer moving through the woods.

Now, back to the particular still-hunt in which faith in an area helped me prevail. I walked quickly up the ridge the first quarter of a mile to reach the best area. The woods were quiet almost to the point of being spooky — the only sound being the dripping of water off the tips of the spruce limbs. I felt a high degree of confidence with the weather, the place, and the rut all being factors in my favor.

Now there are good and bad ways of placing one's foot on the ground while walking on the forest floor. Next time you're out beating the brush, walk a normal shuffling sidewalk gait and listen. Better yet, have someone else do it, and you listen. It's noisy. Then walk by carefully feeling the ground with your feet as they are placed down. Put the heel down first and roll forward slowly to the ball and toes of your foot. It is much quieter.

This simple idea is evidently fairly foreign and difficult to learn for most people. I've been hunting with my young son now for two seasons, and proper foot placement on the ground has been difficult for him to learn and maintain. He got the idea fairly quickly but after a few minutes would lapse back into his usual sloppy, foot-slogging, shoe-destroying gait. (This kid goes through a pair of $28 Nikes every 3 months!) Some of my hunting pals who are good hunters still haven't mastered it.

The idea is to stand in one spot, usually close to a bush or tree to break up the body's outline, and use your eyes to systematically search ahead left and right to the limit of the range of vision. Look through cover and tree limbs and look for deer parts-a throat patch, an ear, or a piece of antler. It isn't often that an entire animal will be seen. Squat down often and look below the brushline for legs or the horizontal line of a back against the vertical tree trunks. Remember, all motions should be slow and deliberate with nothing wasted.

I recently had the opportunity to hunt mule deer in the high, open, semi-desert country of northern Nevada and learned a new technique I think has some merits. My hunting partner for the trip would take off his boots, put on an extra pair of thick socks, and stalk the last 100 yards to a bedding buck in his stocking feet. It was a very quiet and effective method. I have yet to try it but intend to.

When, and only when, the surrounding cover has been thoroughly examined two or three times do you advance. Move ahead only as far as the vision limit of the previous stop and repeat a visual exam of the new piece of real estate. While moving from one spot to the other, examine the

When still hunting look for deer parts — legs, throat patch or a twitching ear.

ground for a step or two ahead with a quick glance. Twigs and other noise making obstacles can be avoided. Forward movement should be made only with your eyes looking ahead.

Often I like to challenge myself by moving so slowly and carefully I don't look at the ground at all. The ground is felt with my feet. If I feel a bump underfoot or begin to hear the creak of a breaking twig, I reposition my boot.

Everyone, even the best, will snap twigs or brush a tree limb from time to time and make noise. The best thing to do is assume your buck heard the noise and stop dead still for several minutes. Snapping twigs are a natural occurrence in the buck's world. He will quickly relax if he doesn't hear any further disturbances.

Still-hunting done properly is exhausting work both physically and mentally. Muscles are on guard to withdraw foot pressure while the eyes and mind search out every nook and cranny within sight. It gives me a funny kind of psychological lift to get so emotionally wrapped up in trying to find a buck before he finds me. It reminds me of the mental and ocular strain that I get when looking through the lens of a camera for hours on end. After finishing a long session at still-hunting I feel like a limp noodle, completely drained. It is a good feeling because I know I've hunted right.

Often, if the area is particularly infested with older, wiser bucks, it is wise to modify the still-hunting technique a bit and do more sitting and watching than walking. Some days I may cover one-half mile all day. It's one way to increase your chances. You will be better prepared to take advantage of any favorable developments while sitting.

By the way, binoculars are a still-hunter's best friend. They condense a lot of ground into a shorter field of view and greatly enhance the ability to pick out deer parts. Also, judging antlers is much easier. Binoculars are a valuable tool and should be used frequently.

I used all these tools on the hunt I'm describing as I worked up the ridge for about an hour — quiet as a mouse. It was one of those hunts I was really getting into. I was thoroughly enjoying myself. I had just stepped to the edge of a small opening. I stopped behind the trunk of a Douglas fir big enough to screen my body and glanced down at my sling swivel, to which was tied my wind indicator, a small piece of frayed dental floss. It was hanging straight down.

Then, incredibly, 30 yards in front of me I saw the final step of a deer as its back leg came to rest. The top of its back and forequarters disappeared behind a small tree. Not knowing what sex the deer was, I pushed the safety off (always carry the rifle in a ready position) and ever so slowly leaned the rifle into the tree as I brought it to my shoulder. I was anchored good and solid.

The deer instantly picked up the motion but because the tree it was behind also screened its view of me, it stepped back and craned its neck high and forward, attempting to see what had moved.

It was a buck! His rack, though not a brush-buster, was good enough, and I had him cold turkey. For an instant our eyes locked. We were frozen in time. I remember his face and neck hair were parted where the rivulets of rain were running off.

The hushed morning stillness was shattered by the roar of my 270. The bullet took the buck behind the angle of his elbow, flush in the chest. He turned to run and fell over, dead.

I don't think I can adequately express the thrill of taking a buck while still-hunting. Essentially, I have beaten that buck at his own game, outdone him with my puny nose and ears. Most of all I suppose it's knowing things were done right — that a difficult hunting method was carried through to a successful conclusion by staying the course through numerous failures. It was almost a spiritual experience.

HORN RATTLING

Antler rattling as a hunting method has come into vogue in recent times. It has been used in Texas for a number of years, but champions of its use have extended the technique into other parts of the country including the Northern Rockies. Rattling may be defined as a mimicking of two bucks fighting with the thought of luring a buck into shooting range.

Personally, I'm not skilled in the method although I have tried it several times with varying results. I do intend to explore antler rattling further in coming seasons.

Many outdoor writers claim antler rattling as a panacea. Just set up, start banging antlers together, and "big horn" comes rumbling in, and he's yours. Not necessarily so. It can, however, bring in big bucks if circumstances and conditions are just right. It is a method that is easy to become discouraged with if a set-up is made on a random basis with no forethought or planning. Rattling should be the brief culmination of a lot of work and study which lays a groundwork to create a successful situation.

Why does antler rattling work? Remember when we talked previously about a buck tending a doe for several hours before and after copulation? As near as biologists can determine, this is the only time bucks fight in a truly aggressive, head-clashing manner.

There are diverse opinions about what the age, size and shape of rattling horns should be. In general, a medium sized, well preserved rack is best.

Rattling in bucks is a fun way to hunt whitetail, but it can be difficult to pull a buck away from cover into an opening.

Bucks are not territorial and do not fight to defend a specific piece of real estate. When another buck comes courting a doe in heat that is being tended by a first buck and the bucks are nearly equal in body size and antler mass, there likely will be a fight. So, logically if an out-riding buck hears the sounds, or simulated sounds, of two bucks fighting, he will respond expecting to find a doe in standing heat and hope for a little action. If the second buck is smaller than the tending buck, a stare or a tipping of the antlers by the dominant buck will run the lesser buck off, or at least encourage him to maintain a respectful distance from the doe. I've encountered this theory in three different reliable sources, and I believe it.

I have been lucky enough to observe the pre- and post-copulation tending activity only once. I was on a photo trip in late November and happened upon a wild buck that was standing attentively looking down into a small depression full of cattails. His posture was extremely tense with head erect and muscles rippling.

Looking into the cattail bog, I spied a doe standing very still. Shortly, she attempted a break-out, coming up to the rim of the depression. The buck grunted and very aggressively, by using sharp turns and rushes, herded the doe back into the hole. The buck really reminded me of a quarter-horse cutting steers.

It just so happened that a few days before I had read about the marvelous way a big buck could be attracted into close range simply by clashing two antlers together in a certain rhythmic cadence, which I had memorized. Consequently, I had myself equipped with a clean, shiny pair of sheds with which I intended to lure in a buck for some close pictures.

Well, I crawled a few yards closer to the buck, and as I did so I noticed another photographer who had evidently been photographing this little scene for some time. He was hunched over a tripod in the deepest concentration, unaware I was around. I squatted in the brush, readied my camera, and held the antlers just like the picture had illustrated. Bringing the antlers together hard (just like the article said) the woods rang with a mighty clash. The buck looked my way, wide-eyed, turned around, and abandoned the doe and left the country. Needless to say, I had a disappointed doe and an angry photographer on my hands.

Not understanding rattling principles or deer biology, my first rattling attempt failed miserably. The buck already had in his possession a doe close to or in standing heat. He wasn't looking to investigate two other fighting bucks.

By rattling when conditions are as right as they can possibly be, real success can be had. Like bugling elk, deer must be in a responsive mood to come in. If the mood is right they will respond to clacking two sticks together. If the mood is wrong, the most expert Texas Hill country rattler will have trouble.

The rutting period must be in full swing. Since mature bucks only fight during the rut and in the presence of a doe in breeding heat, they will not respond to rattling any other time. It will have a negative effect by arousing suspicion.

The buck-doe ratio must be good. Ideally, one breeding buck to two or three mature does is optimum with one breeding buck to eight to 10 does being marginal. The older and more mature the bucks, the better. The idea is competition for a limited number of does by as many breeding bucks as possible.

It appears that wind strength and direction affect rattling success. Successful rattling is almost always done with no or very light wind conditions and early or late in the evening. Often a buck checking the source of the rattling will circle downwind before coming in. This can happen with the hunter never becoming aware a buck was around.

To counteract the scent problems, try to have a line of visibility downwind from the rattling position so the buck must show himself if he tries to wind-check the rattling source. To complicate the matter, it isn't always possible to pull a wise trophy-grade buck across an opening of any size. One way to get around this problem is to buddy hunt. Place a partner 50 to 75 yards downwind from the rattling. He may well catch the buck skulking around.

Personally, I feel masking scents are an unreliable source of concealing human scent. We are a pretty smelly species, and it's beyond my ability to believe that human body odor can be masked by a few drops of whatever. Maybe if our jackets and pants were soaked in the stuff, okay.

Constantly monitoring the wind and applying hunting strategy accordingly is the surest bet. Wearing clean, odor-free clothing helps, too. Masking scents probably doesn't do any harm, but I believe they give a lot of people a false sense of security.

Hunting pressure is another consideration. Bucks that are pushed hard, shot at or are being rattled at constantly are not going to behave in a natural fashion. Pressure will cause the older bucks to become almost totally nocturnal.

To summarize, the ideal spot to set up a rattling station would be in an area where the ratio of breeding bucks to does is good, where deer disturbance has been minimal, and the rut is peaking. Concealment by brush offering a maximum view would place a hunter in good shape. A spot near an active primary scrape in a tree-stand on a clear, windless day would be excellent.

When rattling antlers, the timing of the sequences should be brief. In a natural situation deer don't fight often, and when they do it is almost always brief, lasting at the most several minutes. Try to picture two bucks in a mighty shoving and pushing match and the sounds their antlers might make. First, clash the antlers together as loudly as possible. Then, with the antler tines meshed together, grind and crunch them against each other as forcefully and loudly as possible. This is done for about 30 seconds, at which time the antlers are laid down and the rifle or bow is readied.

After about five to eight minutes, the antlers are worked again. Some guys begin the second stage by just tickling the tines together for a few seconds, while others start again with an attention-getting clash and then repeat the first sequence.

It is generally agreed among the rattling fraternity that the frequency and intensity of the clashes, tickles, and grindings of the rattling antlers are not nearly as important as when and where it's done. Don't become discouraged. Expect failure the first several times and save yourself some disappointment. Stick with the technique long enough and you might

Stay absolutely alert while performing an antler rattling sequence. Be ready for instant action.

When rattling, try to picture in your mind two bucks shoving and pushing and the sounds they would make. In general, rattling sequences should be brief.

have a pleasant surprise. Even super rattlers have slumps.

Dick Idol, a master whitetail hunter and rattler who is a transplanted Texas hunter now living in western Montana, has an interesting philosophy about rattling whitetail deer. He says, "Ninety percent of the bucks slip in to the rattling rather than charge in. The chargers are frustrated bucks which have been run off the does by the dominant bucks. Huge bucks seldom charge in. That's why I really don't advocate rattling as a way to kill the best buck in the area."

Reading between the lines I get two thoughts. The careless, charge-in bucks which afford the best shots are not usually the biggest, most dominant bucks in a given population. The big bucks respond to rattling by sneaking in very carefully under cover and downwind making them very difficult to spot, especially from ground level.

Besides the actual clashing and tickling the antlers together, rubbing them on trees and thumping the ground with ones toes will help simulate the natural situation.

NEXT TYPICAL WORLD RECORD

If you had to guess where the next world record typical whitetail head would come from, where would you guess? The best typical head ever was taken in 1914 in Wisconsin and scored 206 1/8 Boone and Crockett points. Can he be beaten? You bet!

Texas, despite intensive whitetail management during the last decade, had produced since 1974 only one buck large enough to break the magic

170 point figure necessary to be entered in the Boone and Crockett listings.

After researching the subject, I was amazed to learn that Saskatchewan heads the list in total numbers of record bucks taken in North America. The Midwest has always produced trophy grade bucks and with large numbers of hunters pressing the bucks, blind luck may be a factor there.

These forementioned areas are all good bets, but not good enough in my opinion. I would give the nod to my home state of Montana. Thirty-six percent of the 36 bucks which Montana has placed in the record book were taken since 1970. That says good things about the condition of Montana's whitetail herd.

Just one visit to the Big Sky state will tell you immediately why bucks grow old there. There is a lot of remote, high back country where the bucks seldom see a man. People refuse to fight the country. Also, there are lots of other big game species to hunt.

Just yesterday I had a phone conversation with my good friend, Stan Swartz. Stan was hunting elk in September this past season on the Idaho side of the divide between Idaho and Montana. He was at 8,000 feet and glassed not one but three huge bachelor whitetail bucks all living alone in the extremely rugged, isolated country of Idaho's Selway Bitterroot Wilderness. You can bet your home these bucks will have very little human contact as long as they stay high and remote!

Because of the large tracts of isolated habitat in the Northern Rockies, some of which is very densely covered with timber and sliced with rocky draws, the age structure of the whitetail herd is conducive to producing big bucks. The buck to doe ratio is also good since a good many bucks live longer than 2 1/2 years of age.

Probably the most exciting aspect of the Northern Rockies herd is the quality of the genetic pool. Almost everyone I interviewed for this book mentioned this fact. Particular areas within the Northern Rockies have a stronger genetic structure than others.

The extreme northwest corner of Montana and over into the northern tip of Idaho north of Sandpoint contains excellent whitetail habitat and great bucks. Specifically, the Tobacco Valley area around Eureka, Montana, is a good spot. It is a steep, heavily-timbered environment conducive to tree-stand hunting.

Another super area is the Seeley-Swan-Blackfoot Valley complex. The Swan Valley is located between the Bob Marshall Wilderness and the Mission Mountain Wilderness. The country in some respects is more rugged than northern Idaho and northwest Montana.

In the Blackfoot Valley, the country opens up a bit into ponderosa pine habitat mixed with open parks. The north facing slopes of the timbered drainages however, are very thickly timbered.

All the for-mentioned areas have large expanses of public lands and hunting access is not a serious problem.

A 143 1/8 P&Y buck with 22 5/8-inch main beams taken from a tree-stand over a scrape in westcentral Montana river bottom. Greg Munther spent three weeks hunting the same buck nearly every day. He took the buck at a range of 30 yards as the buck was coming in to check his scrape.

To harvest big bucks, one must hunt in areas that hold such animals and use good hunting techniques.

A third area which is noted for excellent bucks is Montana's Bitterroot Valley. Much of the valley floor is privately-owned farming and ranching land where it is necessary to get permission to hunt. The valley is bordered on the west by the Selway Bitterroot Wilderness and to the east by the Sapphire Range. The whitetail's range is extending higher up into both these areas where the land is public. To the west the deer have extended their range to the top of the Bitterroot Mountains and are spilling over into Idaho's portion of the Selway Bitterroot Wilderness.

Still another area which has produced good bucks for a number of years is the Flathead Valley just south and west of Glacier Park.

The Northern Rockies has all the ingredients necessary to produce a new world record: superior genetic pool, excellent quality forage, superior escape cover, and an environment which is helpful in permitting bucks to attain the age necessary to grow trophy antlers.

HUNTING REGULATIONS AND FEES

MONTANA

The general season begins about September 5 for bowhunters. The general rifle season begins the last week of October and runs through Thansgiving weekend. Nonresident deer hunters must purchase a general license for a fee of $450.00. The license is also good for bear, elk, and birds. There are 17,000 nonresident permits allotted on a first-come, first-serve basis (5,600 are designated for hunters who go with outfitters), and both categories go quickly. In 1987, all 17,000 were gone in one day. Contact the Montana Department of Fish, Wildlife, and Parks, 1420 Sixth St., Helena, MT. 59620.

IDAHO

The opening and cosing dates of the general season vary widely, depending on the unit. Some open as early as September while some close as late as December. Check your chosen hunting unit. A nonresident license cost $75.50 plus $52.00 for a deer tag. Nonresident tags are limited to 11,500. Contact Idaho Fish and Game Department, 600 South Walnut, Box 25, Boise, ID. 83707, Phone (208) 334-3700.

Every whitetail hunter's dream.

Chapter Six

THE WHITETAIL MYSTIQUE

Whitetail deer, especially big, mature bucks, frequently demonstrate bizarre behavioral traits. Many times these unusual actions are done as escape tactics, and even though I know better, it almost seems like these bucks are reasoning and thinking.

At any rate, some behavioral patterns are so interesting and unusual that I've decided to dedicate a chapter to them. The following short stories illustrate the cunning and adaptability of the contemporary whitetail deer.

The stories are true and were told to me by the person whose name heads the story. They represent, of course, what has been seen by the human eye. I wonder how many weird occurrences have escaped human detection.

Please note that I intend this as just a fun chapter with no lessons or hidden meanings. Just clear your mind, kick back in your favorite chair and enjoy.

ED WOLFF

It was hot, muggy, and wet. The hunting season was one day old, and I was making a quick scouting trip to check the level of the creek. The next day we planned to float a remote section of bottom-land swamp which was bisected by a shallow, slow flowing creek. Normally, three good jumps would span its width, but recent torrential rains had swollen the creek to three times normal size. Its waters oozed out into the surrounding cypress and bay trees for a distance of 50 yards or better. We hoped to catch the deer bedded on the small, isolated islands of dry ground which represented the remains of the creek's natural banks.

I hurriedly worked my way down off the raised roadbed into the flooded cypress trunks. I would take a quick 10 minutes to check the swiftness of the creek flow and water volume so we could make changes in our float plans, if necessary. I was in such a hurry I made a decision that was to cost me dearly. I didn't take the time to uncase, load, and take my double barrel 12-gauge shotgun.

The water rapidly climbed above my ankles to mid-thigh. My big bitch lab was just beginning to lose her footing and swim. She had fallen about 10 yards behind. As I was nearing the creek proper, I worked my way slowly between the closely growing cypress trees and around small patches of chest-high saw grass.

Suddenly, a few feet behind me there was a tremendous eruption of noise, water, and vegetation. I whirled and crouched at the same time, not having the slightest idea what had happened. My eyes fell on the largest whitetail buck I had personally ever seen in all my years of hunting Florida swamps. The water was so deep the buck had to lunge and jump to make any headway. I could see his beautiful rack and straining muscles very clearly. Then he was gone.

I stood staring in disbelief. Then I put the pieces of the episode together.

Because I'd moved into the swamp so quickly, I evidently had caught the buck in the open as he was moving through the area. He never would have been bedded where I jumped him because there was no dry ground. He apparently had hid by dropping into the water with only his nose, eyes, and rack exposed and let me walk right by. I never saw him. His ruse would have worked except for the dog. That was more than even this crafty old buck could stand.

Another interesting incident happened in the same swamp but occurred during a different season and with a different buck.

It was an unusually cold winter morning for Florida. Paul and I put our heavy jacket and chest waders on and quietly slipped our large innertubes into the slow flowing, tea-colored creek. Snuggling down in the seats slung below the tubes, we pushed off just as dawn was breaking. We planned to spend the entire day slowly floating through the swamp bottom to the next road bridge five miles away.

I really enjoy hunting the swamp bottom, hardwood environment. It is a solitary kind of hunting because not many people enjoy penetrating into the heart of a swamp. I appreciate the solitude. Also, there are lots of deer — old crafty swamp bucks.

We caught several does completely unaware during the first couple hours of our hunt. Each stood up in its bed no more than a few feet from us. They had the most astonished looks on their faces. The creek is small, and we could easily cover both banks from any position with our double 0 buck shot.

Hunting whitetail deer in the cypress swamps of southeastern United States is unique and exciting.

About 2:00 in the afternoon, I heard a dog barking way off in the swamp to my left. Since dogs are used to hunt deer in Florida, I made a mental note to be extra alert. It's not unusual for dog-chased bucks to seek the deepest part of a swamp and to swim creeks to escape the dogs. As we leisurely floated along, I continued to hear the dog on and off for about 30 minutes.

Paul was floating about eight yards ahead of me. I saw him turn his head to say something to me. As his head swung around I saw his eyes open wide and a surprised look came across his face. He started vigorously kicking his feet to turn his tube and at the same time was bringing his shotgun to his shoulder.

I promptly turned my head and looked over my shoulder. A high-racked buck was swimming in the creek 18 yards away. All that was showing were his head and rack. I could hardly believe my eyes.

Paul and I made sure we had maneuvered clear of each other and commenced sending loads of double-O buckshot at the small target offered by the swimming deer.

Paul shot first and the pattern of pellets covered about eight circular feet as it hit the water with the deer's head right in the middle. I shot both my barrels in similar fashion. I could see the deer shake his rack each time the shot shrouded his head, but he kept swimming strongly. Paul fired two more times, emptying his gun.

As I fumbled for my reserve shells in the breast pocket of my jacket, I noticed every time the deer shook its head I could see daylight through his ears. Neither of us got off another shot. The buck hit the flooded bank of the creek and bounded off under a full head of steam.

Since I hadn't yet (and still haven't) learned how to follow a blood trail in water, we were pretty well stuck. We checked for smears of blood on the closely-spaced bay trees, but found nothing. I'm satisfied the buck was unharmed. Had we hit him we would have killed him because the only target was his head. Incredibly, out of five loads of buckshot unloaded at under 20 yards, not one pellet hit a vital part of the deer.

Even more incredible, the buck running from the dog had waited patiently on the flooded stream bank until we passed a few feet away and then slipped his body into the water without so much as making one audible splash. Such is whitetail hunting.

Finally, I would like to relate a story that happened in Montana and was told to me by a friend whose name is Dan Sullivan.

One blustery winter day, Dan was driving down the highway going home and saw a herd of whitetail deer standing in a hay meadow. Dan stopped his rig and began to glass the herd. There were three bucks in the group. As he pressed them to get a better view, the trio of bucks became edgy and began to move out of the field. The bucks disappeared single file behind a low, brushy swell in the ground that was just high enough to prevent the bucks from being able to see Dan or Dan seeing the deer.

The bucks then did a very remarkable thing. They were out of Dan's sight but evidently were still close enough to him that they were concerned about what he was doing. As they traveled along behind the swell one at a time, the bucks would pause, stand on their hind feet so their heads and line of sight cleared the crest of the swell. The curious bucks would get a bearing on Dan then drop down. The entire group then would again travel a bit, then pause, stand, and re-check Dan's position. The bucks repeated the procedure until they cleared the field to the safety of the perimeter of the woods — a remarkable display of whitetail adaptation.

BARRY WENSEL

During the 1984 season, I witnessed three most unusual and unique occurrences concerning whitetail deer.

The first happened in the evening while I was on stand. I had already decided not to accept anything less than a 140 Pope and Young point typical buck or better. It was the first of October.

Four bucks walked past my tree at close range. The first buck was a 4 by 4, the second was a 5 by 4, the third was a 5 by 5, and they all were borderline Pope and Young bucks and would probably score 120 to 125 points. There was a space of about 25 feet behind the third buck — and then a fourth buck stepped out. I promptly did a double-take.

He stepped out at 18 yards and I put the binoculars on him. Sitting on the top of his head was a huge aspen branch with the leaves turned a golden yellow. The main branch of the limb was as big around as a man's thumb. Apparently he had been rubbing his antlers, and the branch locked in his horns and snapped off. The ball of leaves and branches was as big or bigger than a bushel basket perched right on top of his head.

Even studying the buck's head at 18 yards with binoculars, I couldn't see the shape or form of the rack underneath all the brush. I knew he was a good buck because he was bringing up the rear of the four-buck group. His body was half again as big as the other three. I couldn't even tell if he was typical or nontypical.

I've often thought killing him would have been like opening a Christmas present. I would not have known what I had until I untangled all the foliage from his headgear.

At any rate, the third buck stopped right next to my stand and started rubbing his antlers on a small tree when the brush-horned buck walked up beside him. The brush buck nodded his head toward the buck rubbing and seemed to say, "Go ahead and rub all you want Jack, but check this out. I've got the whole tree up here." It was really a humorous situation.

I passed the brush buck over because I just couldn't see how good his rack was. Thinking back I probably should have taken him.

Let me relate a second unusual incident.

I was in a stand (the same stand I had the eight bucks come by the previous year) when a small 4 by 4 followed by a 5 by 5 with a broken bay tine came along. Even missing one tine, the 5 by 5 would have scored 132 to 135 Pope and Young points.

The smaller deer stopped directly under my stand, five yards away. He turned with no aggression intended and faced the larger buck, which was 10 to 12 feet behind. He was carrying his head and rack in a low position, and evidently the larger buck didn't like the display. The bigger buck, with no hesitancy at all, dropped his antlers and smashed into the smaller buck, knocking him right off his feet. He then straddled the smaller buck and repeatedly gored him.

I felt sorry for the smaller buck because he couldn't get out from under the boss buck, which was unrelentingly working him over. Finally the smaller buck regained his feet and took off with the bigger buck showing no inclination to follow. To have such a spectacle happen right under one's feet was awe inspiring. I could have nearly reached out and touched them with my bow.

The victorious buck then did something I had never seen before. He looked in the direction of the departing buck and flared all the hair on his body to an erect position. He looked puffy. He then took a very deep breath and made a prolonged, audible exhaling noise sounding much like the letter V. The exhalation was followed by several deep panting-like breaths. He then looked over toward two does that had been watching the entire scene with an expression that seemed to say, "Did you see that girls? I just whipped the crap out of that guy." My only regret is not capturing the event on film.

Now, I'll relate a third interesting episode that occurred that year.

The date was November 12th or 13th, prime rattling time. The particular tree-stand I was going to set had been used the previous evening by my brother Gene. He told me that he had left a pair of rattling horns in the tree. Since I wanted to rattle this particular morning, I didn't take any antlers with me, expecting to find Gene's in the tree.

As I climbed into the stand in the dark I thought, "What a perfect day it is for rattling. The air is calm, the rut was just beginning to peak, and it's a cold 10 degrees." You could have heard the proverbial pin drop a mile away.

Just after daylight, I looked around and couldn't find the rattling antlers. He had evidently thought he had left them and hadn't. So there I was, facing a perfect rattling day overlooking a primary scrape — but with no rattling antlers.

I sat in the tree about 30 minutes and started thinking. I remembered reading some place where someone had rattled in bucks by clacking two sticks together. Things were kind of slow that morning, and I thought, "What the heck." I grabbed one of my 2219 aluminum arrows and choked up on it so my hand was 9 to 10 inches below the broadhead. I wanted to try to produce more of a clunking rather than a metallic sound.

I then placed the part of the arrow between my hand and the broadhead between the hood of my bow quiver and the limb of my bow. I then vigorously made a circular motion clacking the arrowshaft alternately against the quiver hood and bow limb. This made quite a racket.

I hadn't done this for more than 15 seconds and presto, a 6 by 5 buck ran right in. I passed him up but the point is, of course, I rattled in a buck by hitting an aluminum arrow on my bow.

The moral of this story is to be adaptive. Methods you think are unorthodox or won't work, sometimes do. I have since rattled a second buck doing the same arrow clacking technique. I only wish more of them would come in to the tips of the arrows.

GENE WENSEL

I was hunting with a friend who was putting on a drive, trying to push a buck by me. He was gun hunting, and halfway into the drive I heard him shoot. Soon he worked over toward me and said, "Come here and see this. You aren't going to believe it."

We walked a way through the woods and found a 4 by 4 buck curled up in his bed, dead. He had obviously shot the deer as it was resting. I looked at him and said, "Great, but what's so unusual?" My friend replied, "Gene, when I shot the buck I was standing right here." He was

This buck is at full alert — his left ear cocked forward and his right ear cocked backward.

pointing to a spot on the ground not more than eight feet from the carcass. I said, "What do you mean you were standing there? That's impossible." He then went on to relate his story.

He was moving through this thick area with a lot of brush and hanging limbs. He was bent down low to the ground to negotiate a particularly bad spot. After clearing the thick growth, he raised his head to stand up and saw, a few feet in front of him, this buck bedded down and staring at him. He stared back at the deer rather unbelievingly and noticed the deer had a calm, unalarmed look in his eyes.

My friend hunts with a 30-06 but was unable to shoot the deer because it was like shooting someone's pet. So he stomped his foot on the ground and made a shooing sound, but the deer continued to lay in its bed and gave no notice of being alarmed. It just laid there looking at him. He stomped his foot harder and shooed louder a second time, and still no reaction. By this time my friend was completely bewildered.

Next, he took two steps toward the deer thinking that would cause the deer to do something, but again it didn't. So there he stood six feet away from an very abnormal acting whitetail buck. He still couldn't bring himself to shoot him.

My friend told me he really didn't know what to do next. He didn't know whether to kick the deer to rouse it or what. The awkwardness of the situation made him uncomfortable and certainly consternated.

Then an idea hit him that something was probably wrong with the deer because it wasn't acting normally. He thought, "Maybe I should shoot it to put it out of its misery, plus Gene is never going to believe my story if I don't." So he shot the deer at the base of the neck, left him in his bed, and came to get me.

I don't have the slightest idea why the deer acted the way he did. He wasn't a tame deer as we were miles from any houses, and it was 3 1/2 years old. The carcass appeared normal during the butchering process, and the venison tasted fine.

PAUL BRUNNER

One of the best lessons I've ever learned was during a trip while hunting with Gene and Barry Wensel.

We were conducting a drive through a small patch of very thick willows and quaking aspen. The entire area wasn't more than 40 yards wide and about one-half mile long. On the left side of the thicket was an open hay meadow, and on the right was a 30-foot-tall bluff that leveled off onto a small bench.

I was the driver and was busting my way through brush so thick I couldn't even carry an arrow on my bow string. I was thrashing, tripping and falling my way through more than walking. Barry was up on the bluff looking down into the brush and following my progress. He had a good overall view of the entire scene.

Mature bucks can disappear into cover that doesn't appear able to hide a field mouse.

Stealth and patience is the whitetail's game. Whitetail prefer dense cover as shown here.

I happened to look up at Barry and see him waving his hands and trying to get my attention by making all sorts of gestures and signs. I could see he was very excited about something. He kept pointing and I kept looking at him trying to figure out what he was trying to tell me.

Finally, exasperated, Barry shouted, "You dummy. There is a buck seven or eight yards behind you crawling on his belly." I looked and strained my eyes and never heard or saw the deer.

Barry later told me the buck was a nice five-point, and that he was on his belly doing the Marine crawl, slipping out the back door. The buck had let me walk by at very close range, and then silently vacated the area.

I walked over to where the deer had been and could see the scuffed leaves where the buck had sneaked along the ground. It was a real eye-opening lesson.

DICK IDOL

I was hunting in Alberta, Canada, a few years back and awoke one morning to perfect tracking snow. I knew there was a big buck in the area because I had seen him and his tracks on several of the farms in the area. We located a huge track in the snow which we felt belonged to the monster buck. I told my partners I was going to take up the track. I thought maybe I could pattern him and pin down his activities a little closer.

I tracked him three or four miles through fields, fence rows, and cattle and eventually his tracks led to a little island-like hill with a small pile of cut brush stacked on top. Here he caught me off guard and broke from the brush pile. I never expected him to be in a pile of brushy slash.

Anyway, I took up the track again and while tracking met up with the rest of our hunting group. The deer's tracks led us to another island-like hill top covered with about 60 acres of brush and small trees. We decided the buck was probably in the brushy knob and put four hunters around its perimeter while I planned to walk the woods.

The buck then proceeded to teach me a lesson. His first tactic was to backtrack his trail to see if he was being followed. It was then that apparently he saw us setting up and moved to another corner of the wood patch.

One of the hunters, on the perimeter stands covering one of the possible escape routes, was positioned watching an open pasture full of cows. The pasture was completely open with absolutely no cover, but the buck suddenly appeared between the edge of the cover and the cows. He had chosen to break at just the moment the hunter's head was turned checking the opposite direction.

Before the hunter could recover, the deer ran into the middle of 100 head of grazing cows. The deer slowed to a walk as he worked through the cattle, away from the hunter and toward the safety of the far end of the pasture, never once exposing himself and always keeping cows between him and the rifle.

In the meantime, I was still following the buck's track and just beginning to clear the brush before entering the pasture. I saw where the crafty old veteran had paused, turned back and made double-sure I was still following before he risked leaving the cover for the uncertainty of an open pasture even if it was full of deer-hiding cows.

The rest of the day the tactics were the same. The buck would be one clump of trees ahead of us. Every time we tried to set up he had already vacated the area.

He eventually started running through two or three tree islands between pastures before stopping so we wouldn't know which one to set up on. We lost him at dark with a hearty salute from all of us. We never got a shot at him.

As a matter of interest, the buck made a three-mile loop during the day, and we ended up at dark very near the original pile of cut brush from which I had first jumped him. I never saw that buck again. In retrospect, we should have left a hunter trailing about one-half mile behind the main group to try to catch the circling buck.

Mature bucks have a bag full of tricks and will often do the unexpected to elude the sportsman.

"I've seen and killed big bucks on dozens of occasions and have been in tense situations involving trophy class bucks. I'm no greenhorn, but the second five minutes when the size of the buck's rack became more apparent, my knees turned to jelly. I'm not talking an everyday case of quivering knees but a case of uncontrollable, violent shaking. I actually thought I was going to fall out of the tree right into the middle of the action." — Gene Wensel

Chapter Seven

GENE WENSEL

About three years ago I first became acquainted with Gene through my photography work. He linked me up with Marion James, the editor of *Bowhunter Magazine*. Marion and I have since enjoyed a good working relationship.

I quickly became an admirer of Gene Wensel. Personally, he is very quick-witted and easy going. But as a whitetail hunter, he is absolutely ruthless. He has shown me the true meaning of dedication as I followed his hunting exploits these last few years.

Gene is essentially a one species hunter, pursuing trophy whitetail bucks 24 hours a day, seven days per week. Family and whitetail deer hunting occupy most of Gene's thoughts.

He has authored and published a best selling book, *Hunting Rutting Whitetails*, which has become the standard text in its field. He is called upon often each year to share his considerable knowledge and expertise with fellow whitetail hunters through dozens of workshops and banquets. This is what I personally appreciate most about Gene — his willingness to share freely with anyone who asks the secrets of trophy whitetail hunting with a bow.

Gene will take us on a hunt that lasted through parts of two months. We will be able to follow his thinking and strategy as he gives us a day by day, hour by hour accounting of not only the movements of a trophy buck, but the workings of hunting the same buck as Gene tries to outsmart him.

Even a seasoned, veteran whitetail hunter can get a near fatal, hunt-wrecking case of buck fever if the buck and situation are exceptional.

Gene will tell us about a near terminal case of buck jitters he suffered as the huge Boone and Crockett buck slowly fed its way to and under Gene's tree-stand.

NOBODY IS IMMUNE

The first time I saw the buck was September 28, 1984. I was hunting a ranch in central Montana that is the most perfect whitetail spot I've ever hunted and is ideal for trophy whitetail hunting with a bow.

The ranch has limited access, is composed of classic riverbottom country covered heavily with cottonwood, poplar, and juniper trees with an understory of wild rose bushes, diamond willow and other assorted shrub type growth. On the higher benches, alfalfa, garden vegetables, and some corn is cultivated.

The lay of the bottoms, small breaks, and cultivated sections are such that it is very conducive to whitetail hunting. Aerial photographs show clearly where the deer feed and how travel routes between bedding and feeding areas are arranged.

Another plus for the ranch is that it is located far from any population centers, and having to contend with trespassers is not much of a problem.

I had scouted the property the previous August and my brother, Barry, had scouted it in July. We had learned there were some exceptional bucks on the ranch. The buck-to-doe ratio was good. All things considered, we felt we had a good chance to take a trophy. We both intended to be very selective.

I planned to hunt the ranch in two stages. The first would be in late September and early October and then, if unsuccessful, return for a 10-day hunt during the November rut.

On September 28th, after digesting Barry's and my scouting information and getting a handle on deer movement patterns, I was returning to my truck. I was walking down a crude trail through the heavy riverbottom brush when I rounded a corner and came eyeball to eyeball with a huge buck. We both were surprised and saw each other at the same time. He wheeled immediately and ran. As he swiveled his head to turn, I was struck not only by the general size of his rack, but in particular the length of his tines. I judged him to be near Boone and Crockett proportions and probably a 5 by 5.

I saw the buck at 2:00 in the afternoon. I knew about where he was coming from and where he was going. It appeared he was slowly working his way through the thick brush up to a small bench prior to stepping out at dark to feed on beet tops. I had already located a travel route where the deer were entering and exiting the beet field. Now seeing this buck moving toward that area, I felt he was among the deer using those trails.

I was surprised because the last little bit of cover leading from the bench into the beet field was very open. This is not the typical situation in which

In eastern Montana and Wyoming, whitetails frequent the willow and cottonwood bottoms along rivers and creeks. Tree-stands are a very effective way to take river bottom bucks.

big bucks are expected to be found. Normally they enter and exit feeding through thick cover. Most importantly, however, was the fact I had established the exact route taken by a buck I wanted to collect as he moved to and from his feeding area. I figured the buck was entering the field after dark and spending the entire night there, alternately bedding and feeding. Then just before first light he would start back toward his day bed.

As the trail left the field, it entered a thin strip of very thick brush which fringed the beet field and then passed through the lightly brushed area I mentioned, and finally led to the bedding area in a jungle-like patch of bushes and small trees.

I chose my tree-stand sight in the lightly-brushed area because I could see farther and had good shooting lanes. By the time the deer reached my stand the day would be a few minutes older, providing better light. One disadvantage of the open areas was the trail became less distinct, indicating the deer tended to fan out a bit as they passed through. I couldn't be exactly sure where they would pass.

I chose a tree which I intuitively felt to be the right place and was in my stand well before daylight on October 1st. The stand was 16 to 18 feet off the ground.

An hour after first shooting light had gone I hadn't seen a thing. I sort of expected this. I felt the deer would hang in the fringe brush along the field until the sun broke the horizon and then quickly work through the open

One must discipline oneself to pass over does and small bucks to have an opportunity to take a good buck.

During the rut, breeding bucks are always on the move searching out receptive does.

area where my stand was and into the thick bedding area.

All of a sudden I saw them feeding slowly toward me — six bucks, mostly 3 1/2 years old or older. They were ambling almost in single file. The big buck I'd seen and spooked previously was bringing up the rear.

The odd thing about the situation was the fact that I first saw all six bucks when they were at least 125 yards out. I had an opportunity to watch them for a considerable period of time as they slowly fed my way. One would pass another while still another would step away from the group and smell some curious object. It is highly unusual to watch a hunting situation unfold this way and to keep visual contact with six good bucks for so long.

I have not had what I consider buck fever since I was a teenager. You know, the classic uncontrollable shaking, pounding heart, and weak knees. I've killed and seen big bucks on dozens of occasions and have been in tense situations involving trophy class bucks, so I'm not wet behind the ears. Usually I'm excited but manage to hold things together. Experiencing normal levels of excitement and anticipation is what we are all out there for. It makes for a complete hunt.

The difference here was that almost always the time between visual contact with a buck and my shot is about one minute or less. This is because my tree-stands are quite often in thick cover, and deer seem to suddenly appear. The decision to shoot or not is over quickly. In this case 10 minutes passed between seeing the buck and him being close enough to shoot.

The first five minutes I was okay, but the second five minutes when the size of the buck's rack became more apparent, my knees turned to jelly. I'm not talking an every day case of quivering knees but a case of uncontrollable, violent shaking. I actually thought I was going to fall out of the tree. Holding my bow in my left hand I turned to face the tree, reached up and grabbed a limb in my right hand. The deer were now approaching from my rear. This was fine as I like to have a deer standing broadside or quartering away before I release an arrow.

The closer the buck got to me, the more acute my symptoms became. I think it was a combination of having a monster buck bearing down on me plus the fact that most of the other five would have been very acceptable deer.

The tension became almost unbearable as the first five bucks walked right under my tree. I just knew one of those noses or pairs of eyes would detect me any second and blow my set up. I wanted the big buck so badly I could taste it. I was less than a minute from taking a buck with a bow that would probably score in the Boone and Crockett listings.

I had my head turned so I could look over my shoulder and watch the big buck getting closer. He had five points to a side. I estimated he would score in the area of 170 Boone and Crockett points. He also had one small nontypical point between his brow tine and the base of his antler on the left side. The nearer he came the bigger he got. I tried not to look at the antlers so I could regain my composure.

Meanwhile, some of the other five bucks had cleared my stand while two or three more were still directly underneath me. Picture the situation. I've got a tremendous buck within 50 yards and casually walking closer. Under and around me, some 18 feet away, I've got 10 pairs of eyes and ears belonging to mature bucks threatening to give me away. I knew that in a few seconds the big buck was going to follow the others under my tree. Man, I'll tell you I was fighting the fever bad!

I'm consistently accurate at 15 yards. He was getting close to that range when it finally hit me: I'm going to kill him! But I had one problem. Honestly, I was concerned that if I let go of that limb with my right hand, my knees would collapse and I would fall out of the tree right into the middle of the action.

The buck closed to 30 yards, and as is often the nerve-racking case when hunting whitetails, he abruptly turned and changed direction. He walked toward a small patch of brush in which I knew there was a deer trail leading away from my tree-stand. Immediately I realized there was a quick decision to make which might spell success or failure. Was the buck going to walk over to the brush, feed a little, and fall back in with the other bucks passing under my stand or would he hit the trail in the brush and follow it — not offering any shot? Should I shoot now at 30 yards, my maximum effective shooting distance, or wait hoping the buck would not take the trail and turn back toward the other deer and my stand?

It was one of those now or never situations. To compound the problem I hadn't fully brought my emotions or knees under control. I elected to shoot. The buck was 26 yards away (I paced it off later) walking slowly broadside. I released my white knuckle grip on the tree limb, came to full draw, and let fly. I watched in horror as the arrow, at first centered dead in the middle of his lungs, passed two inches over his back.

Looking back, I feel the duration and tenseness of the moment caused me to lose my shooting discipline. I released my arrow too quickly. I shoot a recurve instinctively, and I simply drew and released a fraction of a second before I was anchored firmly.

I have to admit the emotional letdown was severe — I haven't come that close to crying in a long time. I went from the exhilarating peak of human emotion to the depths of despair in the few seconds it took me to release my grip on the tree limb and shoot an arrow.

I hunted the next three days elsewhere to let things cool down. I didn't want the buck to change his movement patterns. Bucks of this caliber become very nocturnal if disturbed too much. My next opportunity to hunt him was November 12 with the rut nearing its peak. As might be expected, the movement patterns of the deer had changed.

I found the deer were not passing through the open cottonwood country while moving between bedding and feeding areas but had changed to a much thicker, brushy type terrain. They had changed food sources because the sugar beet tops were gone. This had changed their movement patterns. The lay of the land and vegetation types were very different even though my November stand was only 200 yards from my October stand.

I located a primary scrape in a dense patch of brush near a bedding area. I set my treestand between the scrape and the direction from which I figured the buck would approach. He would have to pass me to check the scrape.

I sat the stand the first morning and evening and although several bucks visited and checked the scrape, my trophy wasn't among them. I knew he was in the area and felt confident sooner or later he would show.

On November 13th, I took the stand at 2:30 p.m. At 4:15 p.m., I saw a deer moving toward the scrape. I was unable to see the animal at first because the brush was so dense, but I knew it was probably a buck because he was traveling alone, its body appeared big, and it was obviously moving toward the scrape.

There were three shooting lanes I had cut along the approach route to the scrape. At 18 yards away, the deer stopped in one of the openings with just his rack, head, and part of his neck clearly exposed. I immediately recognized him as the same buck I had missed in October. I knew this because of the one nontypical point he carried on his left antler below his

Tree-stand hunting offers an opportunity to get a a buck into very close range for a high percentage shot.

Taking mature, wiser bucks with a bow is perhaps the ultimate whitetail challenge. Almost all are taken from tree-stands.

brow tine. I couldn't believe I was actually getting a second chance. The sight almost took my breath away. He was magnificent.

As I watched him, he began to rub an overhead branch back and forth across his forehead, completely oblivious to my presence. The seconds passed, and I could feel the excitement begin as one butterfly after another began to tickle my insides. This time I countered by getting mad at the deer. I kept saying over and over in my mind, "I'm going to kill you. You're not going to beat me this time." Psychologically, I was maintaining emotional control by telling myself I was going to take revenge on the buck for what he did to me last time we crossed trails. It was an attempt by me to establish dominance over the deer and control my mental faculties.

All the deer had to do was take two steps forward, and he was mine. I was gripping the string, squeezing the riser of my bow, and gritting my teeth. I mentally said to the buck, "Just give me the opportunity!" I was calm and ready.

He finished rubbing his forehead and stood perfectly motionless for about one and a half minutes. His only movement was to turn his head ever so slightly and look over toward the scrape which he could see from where he was. He could see there were no other deer at or around it.

He then abruptly turned and quartered away from me, keeping several bushes between me and him. I desperately looked ahead of him along his line of travel for an opening. The only one I saw was 50 yards out. It appeared he would pass right through it. The distance made it a very low percentage shot. I quickly debated and declined the shot for fear of wounding him. Sure enough he walked directly across the opening.

About 20 minutes after the buck walked away, I heard a sickening sound — a single gun shot close by, coming from the direction the deer had taken. There were a couple of gun hunters on the ranch at the time. I thought for sure one had blown my buck away.

That night we rendezvoused at the ranch house. I discovered that a gun hunter had indeed killed a deer at 4:30 p.m. in the area where the big buck had drifted off to. To my great relief it was a spike. My big buck was still alive and kicking.

I backed off my stand for two days to let the buck relax and then returned. About 45 minutes after daylight, (the stand was placed closer to the bedding areas so I would have good light by the time the deer worked to me from the feeding area) two does passed right through the scrape and never looked down.

Five minutes later I could see a single deer coming. He stepped clear 15 yards away from me as he approached the scrape. I saw it was not my buck but nevertheless a very respectable specimen. He had five heavy points to a side. I estimated him to be 5 1/2 years of age.

My decision about this buck was influenced by a call I had received the night before from my wife. Her grandmother in Indiana had suddenly died and my wife had to fly back East. Our kids had been left with a babysitter. I'm hard core about my hunting priorities, but in this case I felt a need to go home soon. So time was a factor.

Consequently, I took him cleanly with a single arrow through the middle of his chest. The deer turned and ran out of sight. I heard a crash. I waited 10 minutes in the stand, climbed down, and went to my truck to take off some of my layers of clothing as the day was warming up. Besides the arrowed deer needed to be left alone for a while longer.

It so happened that my brother Barry was in a tree-stand close to my truck. I heard him rattle. I wanted to tell him I was returning home, but decided to wait several minutes so as not to interfere with his rattling.

In due time I walked over to his stand. It was empty. At the base of his tree I could see running footsteps clearly outlined in a light skiff of snow. All of a sudden I heard Barry holler, "Here he comes!" I thought Barry was yelling at me, but I couldn't see anything moving. About 10 seconds later I heard a gun shot.

Later I learned what had happened. The rattling I had heard Barry doing while I was at the truck attracted my big buck to his stand. Again the buck stood behind a screen of brush too thick to punch an arrow through. Just then an approaching doe saw Barry move as he was positioning to shoot the buck, should it step clear. She immediately departed the scene, but the buck thought the doe was running from him. He gave chase, and away they both went.

Barry did take a 35-yard running shot that missed. The arrow passed just in front of the buck's chest.

What I didn't know was the gentleman who has the hunting rights to the ranch, and of whom Barry and I were guests, was set up in a tree-stand 100 yards from Barry's stand in the direction the buck and doe had taken. So Barry jumped out of the tree and chased after the pair in an attempt to drive the deer past our host, who happened to be rifle hunting. And so it worked out — he dumped the buck at 10 yards with a single shot.

My feelings were really mixed. I was happy for our host, of course, because he does appreciate a good buck, but at the same time I somewhat felt, in a sort of odd way, the buck belonged to me. I'd come so close to taking him two times, and felt like we had a personal relationship. We had had two duels, and he had been victorious in both instances.

Later, we scored the buck. He totaled 165 Boone and Crockett points, five short of the book. He was 5 1/2 years old. Since I never had a good head on view of the buck's rack, I didn't realize he was relatively narrow, a 16-inch inside spread, and the lack of spread kept his score a little low of my original estimate. Normally a buck with tines as long and main beams as heavy as his would have an inside spread of at least 20 inches. Nevertheless, he was a beautiful example of his species.

About two hours had elapsed by the time pictures were taken and field dressing chores were done. We then went to find my buck. He had traveled only 75 yards, where we found him piled up. He scored 139 Pope and

Throughout the whitetail's range in the Northern Rockies, major rivers like this provide excellent whitetail hunting in the timbered fringes along the water and in adjacent feeder drainages.

Young Points and had five points to a side.

One final thought I have about the buck fever syndrome. I'm almost embarrassed to tell anyone about the attack I suffered, especially with me being some kind of whitetail authority. But the more I think about it the better I feel. Really, isn't that why we are all out there — to get heart palpitations and all the rest? When the day comes that I no longer get that wave of excited anticipation coming over me at the sight of a good buck, it will be time to quit and retire to my rocker.

Question: Gene what are the primary techniques for taking whitetail deer in the Northern Rockies?

Answer: Our methods are modified because here in the mountains we have the opportunity to hunt undisturbed deer. Deer are more predictable and a hunting set up can be planned around more normal acting deer, i.e., scrape hunting, antler rattling, and trail watching. Rattling is a producer in the Northern Rockies because there is competition among mature bucks during the rut. Again, having undisturbed deer to rattle is helpful.

Question: Would you give us some thoughts on antler rattling and why it is done?

In the Northern Rockies, whitetail deer, particularly bigger bucks, are expanding their range into areas traditionally the domain of mule deer.

Answer: The ratio of mature, breeding bucks to mature does is important as well as the overall numbers of breeding bucks. In short, there must be competition among breeding bucks over the available does.

There is an intangible angle to rattling. It is the mood of the deer. It is kind of like casting a fly over a trout. One day he won't touch it, while on another day, using the same fly over the same water, presented in the same way, the identical trout will smash it. It's the same with whitetail bucks. One day a buck will give the rattling no more than a casual glance while on another day the same buck will come in looking for trouble. What it boils down to is the buck's mood, provided the other rattling conditions are good.

Question: How do you identify a primary scrape?

Answer: I've studied scrapes and hunted them for a number of years. I still have trouble often times figuring them out.

Basically, a primary scrape will have certain characteristics. The soil will appear darker and of a more loamy type rather than sandy or gravelly soils. This is because an organic, less porous, mud type soil will hold the urine odor longer. The physical size of the scrape will be bigger and tend to be located at a trail junction rather than along a single trail. There will be a lot of deer in the general area of the primary scrape and evidence of bedding close by. The entire area will look busy because a primary scrape is a hub of activity.

Question: Gene, why are whitetail deer expanding their range in the Northern Rockies?

Answer: Whitetail deer don't mind altitude even though traditionally they have been thought of as a lowland animal living in heavy cover. When I first moved to the Bitterroot Valley 12 years ago, whitetail deer existed strictly along the Bitterroot River in the bottomlands. They are now expanding their range up the drainages that feed from the mountains into the valley.

I feel they are becoming so abundant they are simply expanding their range. There don't seem to be large numbers of deer high yet, but the ones that are there are the bigger, more dominant type bucks. Other than security, I don't know why the bigger bucks seem to be the segment of the whitetail population seeking the higher type habitat.

Question: How are whitetail deer going to need to be managed in the Northern Rockies, if at all, in the future?

Answer: I don't see any drastic changes in whitetail management here in the Northern Rockies in the foreseeable future. The country here is so heavily timbered and steep, the deer don't get heavy pressure. The big bucks hold tight and let the hunter walk by even at very close ranges. There is a definite need to maintain adequate habitat as well as good winter range. Access needs to be limited, and the sex ratio has to be managed with proper harvests. Essentially, I foresee minimal problems, at least comparably so with other parts of the nation.

"Some of my most memorable hunts have not culminated in a kill. When I think back on different experiences which have been the most meaningful, near misses come to mind. These are oftentimes more emotionally satisfying and rewarding than my kills." — Barry Wensel

Chapter Eight

BARRY WENSEL

Barry Wensel chases whitetail deer in northwest Montana's Flathead Lake country and likes to hunt a specific buck. He will study the terrain, the deer's habits, and plan his attack around the idiosyncrasies of that certain deer which meets his personal standards. Barry is very methodical and persistent, and he is very choosy about his bucks.

Barry is a most interesting person to listen to. He has a way of telling a hunting story that is both exciting to hear but yet is full of useful information. Like his twin brother, Gene, he is always more than willing to share his store of whitetail knowledge with novice, expert, stranger, or friend. Barry is much in demand as a speaker and serves as associate editor of the *Professional Bowhunter* magazine.

Barry relates three experiences any one of which should happen only once in a lifetime but indeed occurred to him in the span of one week's time. The episodes caused him to wonder what he was doing wrong or if he was just losing his mind.

IT COULD ONLY HAPPEN TO A BOWHUNTER

The first incident occurred one afternoon during the first week of October while I was in a tree-stand placed in a riverbottom choked with a growth of alder and willow brush. It was a beautiful fall day. The air was crisp, and the foilage was a blend of brilliant red and yellow colors. I had scouted the area extensively on numerous occasions and knew the movement patterns of the deer very well. I had everything set up perfectly although I must admit, as it turned out, the deer didn't come in exactly like I thought they would.

I had the deer figured to skirt by my stand along the edge of the brush, but I was wrong in that they came by 15 feet deeper into the cover than I thought they would. When I say deer, there were two bucks. Both were trophy class animals with the lead buck actually the bigger of the two. I estimated him to score 150 Pope and Young points and have five points per antler. He was a very decent buck.

The pair stopped exactly where I thought they would, but as I mentioned, were inside the curtain of brush. They stood belly deep in a patch of wild rose bushes. I found the order of the procession to be a little unusual because at that time of year, with the pecking order clearly established, the bigger bucks usually bring up the rear.

The bucks stood broadside approximately 18 yards away. Their direction of travel was from my right to left. The heads of both bucks were turned, looking directly away from me so I didn't have to worry about them picking up motion when I began to draw. Just then, I noticed a dead branch about one inch in diameter running horizontally across the length of the bigger buck's body and positioned about nine yards away or halfway between the deer and myself.

The height of the limb was such that it bisected the deer's upper and lower half so that if I shot above the limb and cleared it the arrow would hit the deer too high in the chest for my liking. If I shot below the limb, I would have to just kiss the bottom of the limb in order to miss it and have the arrow pass above the rose bushes into the deer's lower lung area. It was a tricky shot, and I only had a second or two to decide.

Electing to take the lower shot, I drew and anchored. I was perfectly calm because the action had unfolded so quickly I didn't have time to get a case of nerves. I released the arrow smoothly. It just brushed the top of the one-inch branch and shot straight up and out of sight.

The deer, rather calm for the situation, turned his head and looked in my direction, but didn't spook. Since his gaze was at ground level and under my tree-stand, by using very slow deliberate motions I was able to slip another arrow onto the shelf and nock it. It also helped for me to be heavily camouflaged.

Realizing of course that I'd hit the limb, I knew I needed to bring the arrow down just a pinch. I shoot a recurve instinctively and was mentally feeling my way into the next shot. I concentrated on a spot on the deer I wanted to hit while at the same time subconsciously concentrating on where the branch was.

The obvious happened. I centered-punched the limb, shattered it, and the deer promptly vacated the area. Had it not been for that branch, either arrow would have killed the deer.

Less than one week later, which would be about the 10th or 11th of

This is Barry's best buck taken in 1976. It scored 201 4/8 Pope and Young Points, having seven points on each side.

October, I made another attempt at the buck.

Let me pause in my story a minute to explain a bit of strategy that will have some bearing on subsequent events. Very commonly when I'm hunting with a companion, we will sit tree-stands during the morning and evening hours, then back off to a completely different area to scout or put on a short two-man drive. That way we don't overly disturb the deer in one locale but yet can make use of the entire day, especially the quiet midday periods.

I knew where there was one patch of timber in the riverbottom in which the deer were bedding. It was a very small patch and the wind currents in this particular spot made it extremely difficult to approach. For these reasons, I hadn't hunted this area because I had been alone, although I had kept the idea in the back of my mind.

Anyway, about 1 p.m. on the first day of my return hunt, a friend and I devised a plan to hunt that patch of trees. I took a stand in a ground blind which consisted of me squatting down in a patch of ferns that left my upper torso exposed.

My friend, who is an excellent deer driver, put on a drive through the bedding area. I say excellent deer driver because Rick will put the deer in your lap just about every time. He is just like a bird dog going back and forth, leaving no stone unturned.

Rick moved into the bedding area and pushed a bunch of deer right towards me. Since I was on the ground and the deer came in on me so quickly, I couldn't move. I literally had deer standing all around me.

While the deer were paused getting their bearings, I was able to see a few of them without having to move my head much. My eyes came to rest on a buck that was a 6 by 5 and definitely Pope and Young caliber. I estimated he would score 125 to 130 points. I remember he had a forked bay tine which as a deduct would have made him borderline Pope and Young. He was not the same buck I'd had shot at previously, but still very good.

Standing behind the 6 by 5 was a buck sporting five points to a side and beside him was a 4 by 4. The rest were smaller bucks and does. I recall there was one spike which was standing no more than 12 feet from me.

The whole group started milling around, and as they relaxed becoming less attentive, I could have shot any one of them. Then out of the corner of my eye I saw that the biggest buck was bringing up the rear of the bunch. He came in skirting the rest of the deer, but because I was smack in the middle of the herd, he walked to within 15 yards of me.

Before I had settled into my fern blind, I had picked out several shooting lanes. As luck would have it, the buck stopped broadside and stood perfectly in the middle of one of the lanes and looked away. He was a super buck. His rack was very wide with long tines and five points to a side. I estimated him to score 155 Pope and Young points. Frankly, his

Rick Blas and his big eastern Montana buck taken from a tree-stand during the rut.

Learning the distinctive shape of the whitetail buck's hooves aids in tracking the animal.

rack had a lot of character and was beautiful.

The only thing going through my mind at the time was that I wouldn't get a shot off because of all the other deer so close around me. If I even blinked I would be detected, much less draw my bow. To this day I don't understand why I wasn't winded.

Just then the 6 by 5 that was so close to me turned his head to look at the bigger buck, and by sheer coincidence the rest of the deer followed suit. I took that split second opportunity and drew my bow.

I successfully reached full draw without alarming any of the deer. The rest was duck soup; I had him. I don't want to pat myself on the back, but the fact is I don't miss at 15 yards. I released the arrow clean and smooth. It was heading dead center into the big buck's chest when the arrow suddenly deflected off course. I couldn't even see the twig the arrow hit.

Later when I examined the twig, I saw it was about the size of a thin soda straw. The twig saved the buck's life. This proved to be the one and only chance I ever had at that particular buck.

If all this weren't enough to wreck a guy's hunting season, there's more. Later that very same day I returned to my evening stand in some timber adjacent to an alfalfa field. The tree-stand was in a mixture of cedar and mountain ash trees about 200 yards from the edge of the alfalfa field.

I distinctly remember the sun was still shining, so it was relatively early when I saw the bucks. I wasn't super alert like I am right at dark, but I was watching reasonably attentively.

Now, I don't want to give the idea I was hunting in a game farm or a zoo because the numbers of bucks I'd seen already that day plus the ones I was about to see, I'll admit, seemed unbelievable. I'm honestly relating what happened one day in October, 1984. The entire day I was hunting on public lands.

I've seen other hunters hunt the same land and see only small bucks and does. I don't mean to puff out my chest and brag at all. It's just that I put in time and effort to figure the bucks out. I had the location of my stands carefully picked so as to put myself in a position to see and shoot at trophy class bucks. Again, putting in the time learning the deer and country makes the difference. Anybody can do what I do provided they put forth the effort.

Anyway, I'm setting in my stand and here comes a string of bucks, eight to be exact, walking right towards me. Being righthanded, I position my stands so I can shoot off to the left. The bucks split into two groups at my stand with four going to my left and four going to my right side. None had any idea I was around. I would say five of the bucks were Pope and Youngers, and all were 4 by 4 or better. Two were outstanding.

Two of the smaller Pope and Young bucks passed so close I could have spit on them. Then a 4 by 4 stood 10 yards in front of me. I could have killed him easily except coming up behind him was a big, long-tined, high symmetrical 6 by 6 that I guessed would score 165 Boone and Crockett points. He was very, very impressive but not quite good enough to make the minimum Boone and Crockett score.

He came walking by to my right, and I had to turn in my stand to shoot. Well, the 4 by 4 which was still standing right in front of me to my left and being subordinate to the 6 by 6, had his eye balls glued on the bigger buck. As I watched, the big buck made a move toward the smaller 4 by 4.

Now I had a dilemma. The 4 by 4 was about six steps from cutting the scent trail I had made when entering my stand. I knew my trail was hot because just before the eight bucks had arrived, two does had come by, cut my tracks, and spooked. The 6 by 6 was carrying his rack in a posture showing dominance, and I knew he fully intended to intimidate the smaller buck. As soon as he took a few steps closer to the smaller buck, he would run across my trail and spook, blowing my whole set up.

Remember all this action is occurred in a few seconds time within a few yards of the tip of my arrow.

My decision was this: do I let the 6 by 6 cross over to my better shooting side and closer as he approached the subordinate buck and hope the lesser buck would not run ahead crossing my trail or do I take him at 20 yards off my poorer shooting side before he got any closer to the 4 by 4.

I felt confident I could kill the big buck at 20 yards so I drew and anchored my arrow. I released cleanly just as he walked behind an ash tree limb. You guessed it. My arrow hit a twig that I couldn't even see growing off the ash limb. The arrow buried at the buck's feet.

This buck presents an ideal shot broadside at about 20 yards. His lung and heart area are clearly exposed.

Typical of the timbered country that Barry hunts in northwest Montana.

Later I examined the twig and because of its color and the color of the background behind it, it was camouflaged perfectly. I never saw the twig or, of course, I wouldn't have shot.

The summation of these three hunts are that I had four arrow deflections on what I consider three sure kills on three super trophy bucks. I ended up with three dead twigs. I was very discouraged, but I guess that's what hunting is all about. Sometimes it is almost more than a grown man can take.

One postscript to the eight-buck story. After spooking at my deflected arrow, the deer all ran back the way they had come. The timber was thick, but they stopped where I could still see them. They were confused and obviously didn't know what exactly had happened. The sound of the bow and the thud of the arrow didn't trigger complete panic.

Through a small hole in the trees about 50 yards away, I had a good but limited view of deer parts. I couldn't distinguish any particular deer but wanting to study the bucks again, I raised my binoculars. It happened that I raised my binoculars at just the exact moment to see the biggest buck walking straight away with the second biggest buck also walking straight away, but precisely in front of the bigger buck.

The big buck dropped his head to charge the smaller lead buck, but the lead buck sensed the charge, whirled, and met the larger buck head on. There was a tremendous sound as the two bucks clashed their antlers. They immediately disengaged their antlers, and both deer ran off.

The next time I saw the second biggest buck, he had a broken brow tine on the right side. I'm fairly certain he did it when I saw him clash with the huge 6 by 6. The time lapse between the brief fight and the next time I saw the broken tine buck was two weeks. It is possible he could have broken the brow tine during that period, but I don't think so. The power of the clash I saw was so heavy, I'm certain that's when it occurred.

Question: What do you see for the future of whitetail deer hunting in the Northern Rockies?

Answer: It's good. The terrain in the Northern Rockies is composed of heavy timber and a lot of national forest land. Even though there seem to be houses and subdivisions springing up everywhere, and so-called "progress" taking place, we still have vast amounts of public lands available to hunt. Most of the public lands hold good populations of deer.

In addition, whitetail deer have the remarkable ability to live in man's shadow and do well — in fact thrive.

One thing about the future that does concern me and could possibly affect the quality of whitetail hunting is the ever-shrinking acreage available to deer as winter range. Will these shrinking areas continue to provide adequate nutritional levels to sustain the herds through the critical winter months? Subdivisions in deer wintering areas would hurt the herd. They could either adapt, move, or perish.

Hunting pressure is not a problem in the Northern Rockies. Most hunters are lazy. I hear people complaining the hunting isn't what it used to be. If these folks would get off their butts and out of their pickups and walk 100 yards into the woods, they would do better at taking home venison. The old saying around Whitefish is, "If you've burned two tanks of gas you have had a hell of a good day's hunting."

My point is, because most hunters don't want to get back into the woods and really hunt, I foresee a rosy future for whitetail deer in northwest Montana at least, but I'm sure the same holds true for the entire Northern Rockies region.

Question: Where in your opinion will the next world record typical whitetail buck be taken?

Answer: That's a hard question to answer, and I think it depends on several things. First, I consider the Boone and Crockett and the Pope and Young scoring systems to be designed around symmetry and perfection. In my opinion, that type of a head is in itself nontypical and very rare. There have been some very big, beautiful bucks taken that because of a little symmetry between the two antlers or a few minor aberrant tines failed to make the book. These magnificent animals will never be recognized for what they are.

I'm also a strong believer in genetics and good nutrition. In addition, deer living in northern latitudes have bigger bodies and racks. The combination of northern deer, genetic superiority, and nutrition are all necessary to produce record class bucks.

I honestly feel that somewhere out there is a whitetail buck whose body and antler structure, specifically symmetry, are such that he will be a new world record. He will not only beat the record, he will smash it just as the nontypical record which stood for 90 years or so was recently beaten by a wide margin. Personally I feel the present record of 206 1/8 is way overdue to be broken.

If the most knowledgable whitetail hunters in any one season could line up the ten best whitetail bucks in existence at that time, it would blow our socks off.

In my opinion, the state which will produce the next world record will be a Midwestern one. The agricultural areas of Iowa and Illinois will be high on the list. The bucks produced by these states are short-nosed, big-bodied hogs. They commonly field dress at 250 pounds or better. Their racks are very heavy with good symmetry and lines. All of which pile up points. They are typical of northern latitude deer living on excellent feed.

I might mention other states that have small hot spots. These are Ohio and Minnesota.

I must mention Canada. The whitetail potential in Canada has barely begun to be tapped. We are going to see some eye popping bucks come from the western provinces, particularly Alberta.

Question: What are the two most important ideas for the archer to remember when seeking a trophy grade buck, say 140 to 160 Boone and Crockett points?

Answer: Why only two? There are lots of little factors which separate a buck hunter from a trophy buck hunter. Guys who pattern their methods toward buck hunting are going to see lots of deer. Those which pattern their techniques toward trophy buck hunting will see trophy bucks.

One needs to make up his or her mind which, because trophy bucks must be hunted as a separate species, a breed apart so to speak. They are very different from the rest of the herd. It's like comparing mule deer and whitetail hunting. A person seeking a trophy must gear his thinking and actions in that direction.

A second idea which is important to understand is that most hunters fail to recognize the extent to which a deer uses its nose. People tend to equate their own nasal capacity to that of a deer and because of naivete or ignorance they fail to grasp the truth that a whitetail's sense of smell is manyfold better than their own.

The individuals in a herd communicate mainly by scent. I believe each deer has an individualized odor, much the same as humans each having

A deer's sense of smell must always be considered while hunting or making tree-stand set-ups.

a different name. How else could a doe find her personal fawn when mix-ed in a group of other deer?

There is scent communication among bucks and does at the scrape and throughout the breeding cycle. When a buck rub urinates, he is depositing his personal scent on the ground as a means of communicating to other deer, especially does.

Getting back to your question. If a hunter would realize the acuteness of a deer's sense of smell and how totally they rely upon it to tell them what's going on in their surroundings, he would triple his success rate. Guys splash a little buck lure on themselves and figure it is fine to smoke, not bathe, and ignore the wind. That doesn't get it.

Think about a beagle dog. How does he tell a rabbit is moving left to right? He can't read the tracks, but he can determine by his sense of smell the direction from which the scent is the strongest. Deer are no different.

This deer is Tom's magnificent trophy. It is number six best ever taken and is Montana's number one whitetail buck.

"For years and years I was, out of necessity, a meat hunter. That is how my neighbors and I fed our families. After killing my Boone and Crockett buck, things changed. Now, nothing else satisfies me except the pursuit of record class bucks. It is much tougher hunting but more exciting." — Tom Dellwo

Chapter Nine

TOM DELLWO

Tom Dellwo, a native Montanan who resides in the Seeley-Swan Valley in westcentral Montana, is one of the fortunate few to have killed a whitetail buck with a set of headgear massive enough to be listed in the top 10 in Boone and Crockett — Number Six to be exact. He killed the huge buck in 1974 near his home.

Tom is a hard bitten, tough man who makes his living working with his hands, cutting trees. He epitomizes the rugged, self-reliant Montana outdoorsman. He has lived close to the land all his life and has enjoyed its bounty.

His first rifle, which he acquired in the 1950's, was a 1903 Army-issue Springfield .30-06. It was equipped with a Redfield peepsight with the peep bored out to a larger size. He says it was one of the most accurate rifles he has ever owned.

Tom will share with us two hunts. One describes how his huge trophy was taken and is reprinted as it originally appeared in the 1982 premiere issue of *North American Whitetail Magazine*. My thanks to Dick Idol, author of the original article, for his permission to reprint it here. Tom's second hunt occurred in the 1984 season, and was one in which he was lucky enough to witness an event rarely seen by whitetail hunters.

RECORD WHITETAILS OF MONTANA

Tom Dellwo stood in two and one half feet of fresh, powder snow, studying the wallowed-out trail of what he felt was a large whitetail buck. However, what he didn't know was that this track belonged to a buck that was to be the sixth-largest typical ever entered in the Boone and Crockett Record Book, and the best ever taken in Montana.

Glancing at the slate-colored November sky, Tom wondered about more snow and the short hour of daylight left. "I decided to give him a go," Tom said, "since it was the last day of the 1974 season, and I still didn't have my freezer full of deer meat." Making sure snow wasn't packed in the lens of his old 4x scope, Tom shouldered his Savage .30-06 and took up the trail heading down a steep ravine, which was choked with willow brush and low browse. He knew mature bucks always like to travel these small creek drainages when they had the choice.

"Once," Tom said, "the buck stopped to browse on a clump of snowberry bushes, leaving the telltale imprint of his widespread antler tips in the snow. I wanted to hurry, but after hunting whitetails most of my life, I knew I couldn't afford to make a mistake tracking this one."

"He's heading down from the high country for sure," Tom thought. "The tracks are going in a straight line, southeast." The going was tough because the thick spruce boughs were heavy laden with fresh snow, almost touching the ground. And, going quietly was even more difficult. Visibility was definitely short range. The situation began to look hopeless. The light was fading, and the tracks headed into dense thicket-obviously, it was impossible to slip up on a buck in such a place.

For a few seconds, Tom paused and stared into the thicket — no sign of movement. "What the heck," he decided, "I might as well hit that old skid trail I know heads back toward the pickup."

As Tom rounded the last thick bush, he came to an abrupt halt — a surprised hunter and a huge buck stared at each other! All the snow and hard work was worth that moment.

"Fortunately," Tom said, "the buck was standing in one of the only places I could have seen him — the skid trail. Since all I cared about was putting the winter meat in, I aimed for the neck, so as not to ruin any extra meat. At the crack of the rifle, the buck sprinted away, acting as though he was never touched."

Rushing to the spot, Tom found promising sign on the snow — blood. "That devil can't be too far with all this blood around," he thought.

Two hundred yards later, he realized there was a problem. He could hear a low wheeze each time the buck drew a breath — a grazed windpipe! The tracking went on for another mile, Tom often hearing the buck's give-away breathing but still unable to get in a final shot. "Just at dark, I saw him in the right spot," Tom said, "and I put him down for good!"

It was so dark the hunter only had time to field dress his trophy, prop open the body cavity to cool out, and then hustle back toward his truck. Early the next morning, Tom and his son, Mike, took their horse trailer and a young gelding back to where Tom had left the area that previous evening. Following the trail and finding the buck was no problem. The problem came after tying one end of the rope around the saddlehorn and

Whitetail deer uncharacteristically will migrate to lower altitudes and cover some distance if the snow cover becomes deeper than 16 inches.

the other around the antlers with a half-hitch on the muzzle. The young gelding took about three steps, then looked back and saw "this critter" chasing him.

"Well," as Tom put it, "them two went like banshees through lodgepole thickets, swamps, and whatever else got in their way — straight to the truck."

That afternoon, Tom took care of the meat and threw the antlers into the horse trailer, not finding them particularly interesting. Several days later, a friend happened by and convinced Tom that this particular set of antlers was well above average and should be "scored." Only after this was accomplished did Tom realize what a magnificent rack had accompanied those steaks he had added to the freezer.

This Missoula County buck was the new No. 6 typical in the all-time records of the Boone and Crockett Club and highest-scoring typical ever taken in Montana, with an official score of 199 3/8 points. The 13-pointer had a spread of 24 inches, and the main beams measured over 27 inches in length. The buck also won first place at the "Sixteenth North American Big Game Awards" in Denver in 1977 as the best typical whitetail entered in 1974, 1975, and 1976. Today, Tom is a trophy hunter. He looks at steaks and antlers in a different perspective now than he did back in '74.

To my knowledge, only three or four states in the country can lay claim to having produced two typical whitetails that place in the Top 10 of the Boone and Crockett records, and Montana is one of those.

When most hunters think of Montana, their minds automatically jump from elk to mule deer, to bighorn sheep, to bear, and to antelope. Only

A trophy is in the eye of the beholder. On the left wheelchair-bound Bruce Burk looks on as his uncle Stoney capes Bruce's first whitetail.

then may they think of whitetail! However, today, even the most casual observer would agree that interest in whitetail hunting, especially for trophy bucks is at an unprecedented all-time high.

Why, then, are more hunters not "tuned in" to the Montana whitetail? Obviously, one of the major reasons is Montana's geographic remoteness. It's a long way from anywhere! You don't drive over from Pennsylvania, or up from Texas, to hunt the weekend, unless you are "driving" a plane. Another reason is that there are no major population centers, such as Denver or Spokane, which concentrate hunting pressure and lead to more exposure. Montana boasts a whopping 800,000 human population which is fewer people than one of Pennsylvania's larger cities. With Montana being one of the largest states in the U.S., hunting pressure is relatively light, statewide, and very light on a per acre basis.

Also, the interest in whitetail trophy hunting hasn't blossomed yet in Montana. The locals seem to prefer going after the "economy-sized steak package" — elk, or the more visible mule deer. Those old whitetails just don't seem to cooperate too well when it's time to fill the freezer! Even the Montana outfitters and guides haven't placed any special emphasis on the "super" bucks. One still sees the ad "elk, deer, and bear hunts" with no emphasis even placed on what kind of deer. Consequently, there are very few options open for guide service for trophy whitetail hunters.

As far as whitetail hunting is concerned, Montana is made up of two distinct geographic areas — eastern and western. The eastern region, which comprises roughly two-thirds of the state, is basically big expanses of open plains, low mountains, and large ranches. The two large river drainages, the Missouri and Yellowstone, and all their tributaries are a distinct plus for whitetail hunters. The massive cottonwoods and various types of browse along the rivers provide the basic cover for the whitetail. The deer often leave this riverbottom protection to feed or bed in the rough "breaks," the many washes and gorges that have carved the terrain from the higher plains down to the low riverbottoms. As with most whitetails, they generally live in a "square-mile" home range, although this occasionally expands if food or cover is lacking. These large-bodied deer belong to the "Dakota whitetail" subspecies (Odocoileus virginianus dacotensis), with those in Montana being in the most western fringe of the subspecies.

In contrast, western Montana looks as though it came straight from a postcard collection. The spectacular Rockies, covered with massive ponderosa and larch pine and emerald-clear streams and lakes, have a beauty that will rival that of any mountain region in the world. This predominately public land has some cattle ranches, but they are relatively few because of the limited amount of pasture.

The "northwestern whitetail" subspecies (Odocoileus virginianus ochrourus) inhabits western Montana, Idaho, Washington, Oregon, California, Nevada, Utah, and the Canadian provinces of British Columbia and western Alberta. This subspecies has a winter coat that is a rather pale brown, as opposed to the darker coats in the central and eastern parts of the U.S. When one "strikes off" after the western whitetail, he is definitely confronted with some unique problems and situations that he is unlikely to face in other parts of the country.

Who has ever heard of whitetails migrating? Well, in western Montana some of the whitetails travel anywhere from 15 to 70 miles. Now, I know you're thinking "How do they know?" For several years, the Fish and Game Department of Montana has been doing a study on whitetails in specific regions in order to learn more about their habits and ecology. When several whitetails were harnessed with radio-equipped collars, all suspicions were satisfied as most of the deer migrated many miles.

Basically, the reason for migration is that both elk and deer are forced to leave the higher elevations, because of deep snow, and move to lower elevations where the snow levels are more moderate. When the spring thaw occurs, the deer generally migrate back to their home range. The reasons for migration are complex, but the fact remains that the majority of whitetails in western Montana do migrate — making a particular trophy buck even more difficult to hunt.

Coupled with the complexities that migration poses, the heavy timber and cover make it difficult, especially for the inexperienced hunter, to "pattern" a particular buck. This is very important to a trophy hunter since he must learn where "his" buck beds and feeds, which trails the deer uses most often, and basically determine the boundaries of its home range. This is not always easy. For example: a buck's bedding area is on a thick plateau at 4,500 feet elevation. In late afternoon, he leaves this area and travels down to a thick creek drainage, sitting at 1,500 feet elevation, arriving after dark. Before daylight, he works his way back toward his bedding area, using the thermal currents to his advantage the whole while. With all the country between these two areas, you can see how difficult it is to pin down a buck. Even the terrain itself can be a problem since this is rough country, requiring good physical condition to traverse the mountains all day.

Something that is unique in western Montana, although not a problem, is the diversity of big game. While hunting whitetails, one might see elk, black or grizzly bear, mule deer, bighorn sheep, mountain goat, moose, or even an antelope. This certainly increases the hunter's odds of success for some kind of game. All of these unique problems and situations contribute to a great challenge and mystique when searching for a trophy Montana whitetail.

Yes, Montana has produced a couple of the finest typical whitetails that have ever been taken, not to mention the other 19 typicals and 17 non-typicals currently listed in the Boone and Crockett records (36 in all) from Montana as well. And often, as I am perched on a particularly panoramic view point, I gaze out across hundreds of square miles of prime whitetail country and wonder, "Which drainage is home of the next world-record typical?"

I actually had a more exciting hunt in late November during the 1984 season than the hunt on which I took my trophy.

It was November 22 with just two days left in the season. The morning kind of reminded me of the day I took my big buck. The conditions were even the same. The snow was deep and the temperature about 15 degrees.

I planned to drive my pickup as high as the snow would permit and then hike up from there. I was going to hunt an area in which I often saw good trophy grade bucks.

It's been my observations through the years that certain small localities seem to produce monster bucks. These small areas may even be surrounded by a larger area that in themselves are noted for big bucks. In other words, there seem to be certain spots within areas that have a superior genetic strain of deer. To illustrate my point, I have seen only one buck bigger than my trophy, and I saw him in exactly the same area I killed my big buck but several years apart.

Outstanding bucks come very hard even after a hot spot has been located. The secret is to put in lots of time in order to figure out a buck . One method I use to locate good areas is to look for shed antlers. I then can plot deer movements as well as see physical proof of what classes of bucks live in the country in question.

The big trophy class bucks are older bucks that have had human experience before, probably unpleasant experiences. They hang back in the thick brush and deep snow, showing themselves infrequently. They make few mistakes.

The idea is not to skip all over the country looking for big bucks. Find a spot that has good bucks and learn the country like your living room. Hunt often and hard.

Just after daylight I was nearing the end of the road when my truck

This buck traveled over 25 miles and dropped 2000 feet in elevation to reach a snow depth he could survive in.

started to lug down in the deep snow. I happened to look up the ridge, and I saw a white flag bouncing away through the heavy timber. On the other end of the flag was a very good set of antlers.

I parked the truck and eased my way up the ridge in hopes of seeing the buck or at least locating his tracks. I was quickly disappointed. The entire hillside was crisscrossed with dozens and dozens of deer tracks and trails. Sorting him out would have been impossible.

I crested the ridge and had a feeling the buck had done likewise and was in the timber just below me. While contemplating the situation, I heard an electrifying sound which captivated my attention. My mind immediately identified the clacking, grinding sounds as those of two bucks fighting.

I looked to my left and 150 yards away were two very respectable bucks engaged in a mighty shoving and pushing match. It was one of the most dramatic and impressive events I'd ever seen during all my years in the woods. I stood transfixed, watching as the two bucks grunted and shoved each other out of my line of view. They disappeared behind a wall of timber and a churned-up shower of snow.

Now I debated — do I go after the two fighting bucks or sift through the timber ahead and try to jump the original and biggest of the three bucks? My problem was suddenly solved as the single buck did indeed prove to be in the timber below me. At 200 yards he broke clear of the trees for a split second and I fired, missing. He disappeared and I glanced toward the fighting bucks just in time to see their flags waving goodbye. I had no venison that day but I did have a wilderness memory to add to my mental album.

Question: Tom, how have your hunting methods changed going from a meat hunter to a trophy hunter?

Answer: I first select an area that has trophy bucks rather than wondering randomly through the woods. I then still-hunt and read sign as I go. I'm not reading sign to learn the area. I've already done that before the season. I'm reading sign to bring me up to date concerning the most current deer activities. Most importantly, I'm more patient than I used to be and that is critical. I sit a lot more than I used to and this greatly improves my chances of collecting another Boone and Crockett trophy. Staying alert is necessary too. Big bucks will give you one quick look and then go hard and far. They are expert at putting the available cover between themselves and the end of a rifle barrel.

Question: When you first walked up to your trophy, what was the first thought that went through your mind?

Answer: You won't believe this, but I felt disappointed. I was strictly a meat hunter at the time, and the buck was small bodied and run down. Antlers meant nothing to me. I'd hang the racks of bucks I'd killed in the trees for the birds to pick clean, or I threw them to the dogs. I'm sure over the years, my dogs enjoyed some mighty high classed bones. I remember thinking, "Damn, I've killed a deer that's all antlers and testicles." I have since changed my attitude.

Question: Tom, you are a dedicated hunter and have hunted whitetail deer nearly four decades in an area which is famous for producing trophy animals. You also work in the woods for a living. How many bucks have you seen that would meet or beat the 170 points necessary to be listed in the Boone and Crockett records?

Answer: A grand total of four including the one I harvested. My boys, who are 23 and 25 years of age and hunt long and hard every season, kill bucks every year. Their bucks are just missing the book by eight to ten points. I will predict a Dellwo will put another whitetail buck in the Boone and Crockett records in the next two years.

Question: Whitetail deer are usually not thought of as being migratory. Your trophy appeared to be moving downward in a direct line toward the southeast. Where was he going?

Answer: In our country the winter seasons are very tough with deep snow and severe cold. My buck waited until the snow was 2 1/2 feet deep before lack of forage forced him to move down. I might add,I first cut his tracks at 5,000 feet elevation, and there were no tracks of any kind higher than his, not even elk. He was on the east side of the Seeley-Swan Valley in the Swan Mountains and migrating 25 miles to his wintering grounds near Boyd Mountain.

Dick displays one of his trophies—a huge nontypical buck.

"Number one above all else, a hunter has to hunt in a place where big bucks exist. Most hunters don't have the option we have here in the Northern Rockies. So they need to do their homework and research and define the places where the biggest bucks are found. Every state, whether it is Florida, Michigan, or Alabama, will have certain areas that produce bigger bucks than others. They may not be Boone and Crockett bucks, but the deer will be the best the state can produce." — Dick Idol

Chapter Ten

DICK IDOL

Dick Idol is many people wrapped into one, but first and foremost he is a whitetail man. His credentials are impressive.

He has numerous articles published each year in outdoor periodicals, among them *North American Whitetail*, of which he has served in the past as research director and is the co-founder. The magazine is devoted to the serious whitetail hunter.

Dick has probably the most balanced, total collection of whitetail antlers in the world, some of which are caped and mounted. The collection includes 30 Boone and Crockett trophies both typical and nontypical, as well some hundred plus freaks, oddities, and rare racks. It is a collection that absolutely takes one's breath away. Animals demonstrating either superior massiveness, spread, main beam and total tine length, and numbers of nontypical points are all represented in the collection. Many of the bucks have all the above qualities.

Idol started collecting fifteen years ago when a particularly large rack stored in a barn caught his eye. He paid $25.00 for it.

Dick conducts many whitetail seminars and fulfills numerous speaking engagements every year. He is much in demand and will spice up his presentation by showing some of his heads. He has hunted whitetail deer since he was a young boy, and now in his early forties spends many weeks each season hunting trophy bucks across North America. During the 1984 season, he collected a trophy buck in Texas that had nine total points and a 22-inch spread, a Saskatchewan, Canada, buck with 12 nontypical points, and a Montana buck that totaled 11 points. He also chased a nontypical Alberta, Canada, buck with a huge, club-shaped dropped tine for two weeks and only saw him once.

At the conclusion of our interview, I asked Dick if there was any final thoughts he would like to express. He replied: "Yes. Every year I'm becoming more and more concerned about the ethics of the hunt, and the conduct of the men in the whitetail fraternity. There are some people who are losing sight of what hunting is all about — namely enjoyment, excitement, and personal challenge. It appears the whitetail phenomenon is growing rapidly, and personal advancement up the prestige ladder and standings in the record book should not be put before the very things that made whitetail hunting the number one hunting sport in North America!"

Dick will take us on two hunts. The first is a Texas hunt on which a big buck's habit of preferring dense cover actually worked against him. The second concerns a big Montana buck collected only after a dawn-to-dusk hunting and tracking marathon.

TABLES TURNED

This hunt occurred in 1977 or 78, I've forgotten, and it's one that I've never published anywhere before.

I had been hunting and guiding in south Texas for two years and had leased a ranch in order to provide quality guided hunts for my clients. The ranch was large and in previous seasons had been hunted quite a bit by its owner. Consequently, we hadn't seen any really big bucks, although I had sighted several good bucks. The ranch was in a part of Texas noted for exceptional bucks, and in the past it had produced two or three Boone and Crockett heads. The properties on either side of the ranch were closed to hunting and held big bucks and that is why I would see big bucks moving in and out of our hunting area.

The ranch was typical south Texas brush country. The terrain is flat with a lot of pear cactus, mesquite, and both black and white brush. The ground cover is very dense and thick on good portions of the ranch. The country is arid, but the landscape does have a green shade to it when viewed from a distance. The few trees are usually less than eight inches in circumference. There are lots of cattle and their beaten trails spiderweb the ranch.

As far as hunting techniques, tower stands are used a lot to get the hunter above the brush level. Ground stands are set up to watch the senderos which crisscross the country. Senderos are cleared, straight pathways through the brush and resemble road beds. They intersect each other at intervals and run for miles. They are used for oil exploration. Since there aren't many natural openings in the country in which deer can be seen, sendero watching is a popular hunting method. Stands are set where the deer travel past them as they move along the cleared swaths.

I had been guiding and hunting the ranch for about three weeks, and it had come down to the afternoon of the final day of the season. I found

Whitetail deer prefer densely vegetated areas like this where escape to cover is close by.

myself in a remote back corner of the ranch having dropped hunters off at various stands as I moved through the country. I had never hunted this section of the ranch before. Stretched out in front of me was a sendero which led down through a slight bottom and up and out the other side. In the bottom was a heavy growth of white brush that grew along the course of a dry creek bed. The brush and creek bed intersected the sendero at a right angle.

White brush has a whitish appearance when seen from a distance and grows in impenetrable clumps. It is the densest and closest growing of all the types of south Texas brush; the thickest of the thick. It is however, one of the few types of vegetation that doesn't have thorns and consequently deer like to travel in it.

I picked out a place in the sendero where I could watch the point at which the white brush intersected it. Any deer traveling the brush would momentarily be exposed when it crossed the sendero to re-enter the brush on the opposite side. The crossing point was 300 yards from my stand.

My stand was really a last ditch effort on the last day of season at the far reaches of the ranch. Strangely, I had a good comfortable feeling because the set-up looked so good, and the country looked bucky. You know, it's a feeling you sometimes get that things are going to happen.

River bottoms throughout the Northern Rockies provide some of the best big buck potential for serious whitetail hunters.

I sat down, and about 4:30 a doe followed by a buck stepped out of the bottom and looked down the sendero. I quickly glassed the buck and remember thinking to myself what a nice animal he was. Before I could commit myself to a shot, both deer stepped across the sendero and into the white brush. The doe was obviously in heat and being followed attentively by the buck.

I sat there trying to second guess myself. Should I have snapped off a shot or should I run down to where they disappeared? My thoughts were abruptly interrupted as a second buck walked out in the exact spot the first one had. I put the glasses on the second buck and whistled to myself softly. There stood the best buck I'd ever seen on this ranch. His rack extended four inches beyond his ear tips. The buck, before I could lower my glasses, glanced up and down the sendero and disappeared into the far side of the white brush.

Normally your chances are over at this point when hunting in the Texas brush country. Once a deer gets out of a sendero into the brush, I won't bother with them. It's an impossible situation. This time, since that was the last opportunity I would probably get that season and the buck was so good, I decided to try to get him. Jumping to my feet, I ran to the spot where the buck had gone into the brush. Actually, I stopped about 40 yards short of the deer's entrance point.

My plan was to walk parallel to the deer as they traveled down the 40 yard wide strip of white brush and attempt to find some kind of hole to punch a 30-06 slug through. The deer were moving in the strip of thick brush along the dry wash while I was along its edge in slightly more open country. The ground was pounded flat by cattle hooves, so I had relatively quiet going. The wind was quartering from me to the deer so I knew I would have to stay ahead of them.

As I worked the edge of the brush parallel to the deer, I could hear the two bucks' antlers popping against the dry white brush as they tracked the doe. As I sound-tracked them, I was struck by the role reversal. It was the first time I had ever had an opportunity to beat a buck at his own game. Here I was hunting and tracking with my ears. The three deer had no idea I was around.

After covering 100 yards or so, I still was unable to catch even the tiniest glimpse of hair or horns even though I was 30 to 40 yards from the bucks. I must say the excitement and tension epitomized what deer hunting is all about.

The first buck I'd seen cross the sendero was, I was almost certain, a 5 by 5, and the second and biggest buck was a 6 by 6. Naturally, I wanted the bigger buck, and if I could find a clear window in the brush I knew I could distinguish the two.

Finally, I saw a patch of brown hair. Above the hair I could see an antler beam with five points. I didn't shoot, but walked along again 30 to 40 yards, hearing but not seeing. By now I was suffering a severe case of eye strain; in fact, all my senses were super tuned. While doing all the looking, I had to be careful where I placed my feet. One twig snap and it was all over.

Again, another piece of a body popped out through the brush. This time I could see that the beam attached to the fur had six points on it. Even with my limited view I could see the deer's body was tensed and frozen in position. He wasn't looking at me, but he had either sensed me or had gotten my wind. I felt a strong wave of urgency that his would be my last chance.

Through the brush I picked out a spot of fur in what I judged to be the chest area and shot. There was a tremendous crash as all three deer took off. Almost immediately the biggest buck broke out of the white brush ahead of me and disappeared out of my line of view.

I waited and waited and heard or saw nothing. My mind raced back over the shot. I was very close to him when I squeezed off and felt he was hit, but the brush was so thick that I knew the bullet could have deflected. All the Monday morning quarterbacking was going through my mind as it always does in these situations: what if, maybe, perhaps?

After 20 minutes I walked over to where the deer had been standing when I shot and found a little blood and hair, but not much. I felt better, relieved in fact. I at least now had a chance of collecting him. I followed the blood trail to the point at which the buck had exited the white brush and found lots of blood. I continued following the blood about 60 yards and came to an area where the country opened. I could see ahead for a good distance. Feeling he was dead, I scanned ahead but couldn't see him.

I felt a tiny knot of worry creeping into my belly and left the blood trail and scrambled ahead trying to sight him. I had about 30 minutes of daylight left and felt the sick panic feeling creeping higher in my gut. I really didn't want to lose that buck, but I couldn't see him anywhere.

I regrouped and went back to the blood trail and began to track him out slowly. I'd no more than taken a few steps, and there he was. I had been standing almost on top of him all the time. He was piled up in the middle of a small patch of brush he had evidently tried to jump and died in mid-jump. He was stone dead in the middle of the brush pile.

The buck turned out to have a 6 by 5 rack with a 23-inch spread and scored 160 Boone and Crockett points. He was a nice deer taken after an exciting, difficult, 45-minute hunt. It just so happened that I'd made all the right decisions this time. The hunt sort of made up for some of the bad decisions I'd made on previous hunts.

Dick Idol's 29-inch-wide, 13 point monster. Note this buck's extraordinary spread.

ALL DAY BUCK

I was hunting a specific buck, in fact, two specific bucks. My brother and I were hunting on a ranch in eastcentral Montana that we had scouted previously. One of the bucks I had my eye on was typical, and the other carried a nontypical rack. The typical buck I had actually seen and judged, but I had only found the nontypical's shed antler. I had scored the shed and doubled it for a total score of 238 Boone and Crockett points.

I really preferred to take the nontypical if possible, but during my four or five days of scouting I'd looked at a lot of bucks and had seen a couple of typicals that would be very acceptable. Most of my scouting time was spent sitting at various vantage points and using binoculars.

On November 5, I met my brother at the ranch to try our luck. The bucks were still running together as the rut really hadn't started.

One of the typical bucks that I was interested in fed and bedded regularly in a thick patch of brush enclosed by a bend in a small river which flows through the ranch. The river course passes at the foot of a 30-foot-high bank overlooking his feeding area. Just at first light I slipped up the offside of the bank and peeked over the top.

It was 18 degrees below zero that morning. I can remember how hard and cold the ground felt as I crawled the last few feet to the top of the bluff. There was also a very light skiff of powdery snow on the ground.

My sneaking and crawling weren't good enough because the first thing I saw was a doe hightailing out of the country. All of a sudden, directly below me I heard a crash followed by the clacking of brush against a running buck's antlers. The sound was close but the brush was so thick I couldn't see the buck.

I followed his sound for a few seconds when he broke into a less dense patch of brush where I could see him for the first time. For a fleeting second, my eyes riveted on his heavy, tall rack. I then slid the crosshairs down to the base of his neck and shot. He didn't go down or even flinch as he ran back into heavy cover and disappeared.

My brother commented, "I think you got him." The next thing we saw was a deer 250 yards out and running. He entered a piece of cover and stopped. I immediately knew it was the buck I had shot at. I leveled my rifle, and not having a place nor the time to take a rest, shot offhand. He vanished.

About one minute later at 400 yards out he broke again, running full tilt heading into the breaks above the river. I glassed him and saw he had unfortunately suffered a broken left rear leg. Every so often he would stop to look back at us as he worked higher into the rough, gullied terrain and then went out of sight over the top about three-fourths of a mile away.

We gave him an hour and then went to pick up his trail where I had originally shot. There was no hair or blood to indicate I had hit the buck with my first shot, so we started tracking him with the help of the light skiff of snow. We worked our way over to the second place I'd shot and found some hair and blood so I was able to determine my second shot was the one that connected.

We were able to easily follow a light blood trail that led us to the point where we had last seen the buck go out of sight over the top of the breaks. As we reached the top and looked over, we were staring into a 20-to-30 acre, more or less enclosed, lightly-brushed basin with small coolies leading into it. My brother and I glassed and glassed into the dead-end basin but couldn't see the buck.

Finally, the buck's resolve broke, and we saw him going up the other side of the bowl heading for the top. He stopped on top and looked back at us. I thought about shooting, but he was over 300 yards out, it was very cold, I was breathing heavily, and there was no rest nearby so I held my fire. Then he was gone over the top.

My brother and I reached over to the last place I'd seen him and couldn't believe our eyes. Five hundred yards away we could see the buck going back into the river bottom. I could see he was slowing down, but he wasn't' going to leave his home range even though hard pressed.

This is an important whitetail characteristic to remember when hunting a specific animal or tracking a wounded one. Whitetail deer are very reluctant, even under the most stressful situations, to leave the territory they are familiar with. Deer prefer to take their chances in a familiar habitat. Sometimes when tracking a deer that knows you are on him or a wounded one, it is wise to have a companion trail you about 100 yards back. He just might catch the buck doubling back.

The buck entered a terribly thick crawl-through, five-acre brush patch and again disappeared. We gave him another hour hoping he would weaken further.

We then went to the point where the buck had disappeared, and leaving my brother, I worked to the other side of the brush across the creek and set up. Our plan was to have my brother bird-dog the jungle and try to flush him my way.

My brother entered the brush, following an even more faint blood trail that soon stopped altogether. After a few minutes I heard a loud crash and my brother said, "Here he comes!" I instantly was on the keen edge of excitement, rifle at ready, and straining to see the buck. I heard the deer hit the ice on the creek. As I put my rifle to my shoulder, the deer came out of the brush. He was a big buck, similar to the one we were tracking except for one thing — he wasn't limping. He passed me at 30 yards, broke into the opening brush, and shifted into high gear.

I yelled toward the sound of my brother thrashing in the brush, "Wrong deer. Keep going."

Incredibly, about two minutes later I again heard the brush popping and crashing in quick rhythm. A second similar-looking big buck appeared following the exact path of the first. His body was even bigger than the first

A late winter buck which scored 145 typical B&C points.

The advantage of a tree-stand is depicted here as this nice buck is totally oblivious of the hunter's presence.

buck, but again the second buck wasn't limping. Wrong deer again!

I yelled a second time to my brother, "You aren't going to believe it. It's not him. Keep thrashing!"

By this time we were beside ourselves. We couldn't figure what the heck was going on. In fact my brother was about to have a grand mal seizure. I wasn't far behind. Where was our buck?

It was now 4:30 in the afternoon, and we were tired, and cold. The blood trail had dried up, and the skiff of snow had melted. We were going basically on our instincts. My brother again began crisscrossing the dense brush in a desperate effort to flush our buck.

Finally, he walked close enough to the buck that he could see his bedded outline through a screen of brush. The buck cracked and broke with a crashing of brush. Later I asked my brother how he had found the buck with no blood or snow. He related that between a rare speck of blood, a small unmelted snow patch here and there, scuffed ground, and turned-over pebbles, he was able to painstakingly track the deer to its bed.

When the buck broke cover, I was standing on the far side of a frozen beaver pond bordered by a one-yard-thick strip of brush that was itself bordered by an open sage brush flat. I chose this spot because I felt the buck would try to escape by crossing the creek and travel in the strip of cover to avoid open sage brush.

I heard my brother scream, "This is him this time. Get ready!"

Rather than cross the frozen creek like I expected, the buck crossed it below me on the beaver dam. Not having a clear view, I was unable to shoot. The buck crossed the dam and once across had difficulty negotiating the high creek bank, but did so and vanished again. I waited for perhaps fifteen minutes for the buck to come through the brush to me, but he never did.

My brother worked his way to the beaver dam, looked at me, and shrugged his shoulders. I looked at him and shrugged my shoulders in bewilderment. No buck. I pointed north, the only way the buck could have gone without me seeing him. Had he gone south he would have passed me in the brush strip I was in. If he had chosen the open sagebrush, I would have seen him.

My brother then noticed a good blood trail on the beaver dam. Moving through the rough brush had started the buck bleeding again. He tracked him to the top of the opposite creek bank and was now on the same side of the creek as I was but 60 yards downstream.

He noticed the blood trail turned toward me, so the buck was between us after all. Now let me clarify the picture. My brother and I are both standing in a 15-yard-wide strip of short brush bordered on our right by the creek and on the left by an open sagebrush flat. We are 60 yards apart with the buck somewhere between us. In fact, I could even see my brother.

My brother started moving toward me following the blood. In a few seconds he yelled, "Get ready; he's coming your way hard!" At 40 yards I saw the buck in front of me and heading towards me. He ran along the edge of the sagebrush 15 feet from me, and I ended our hunt.

He was well worth the effort. The buck field dressed at 215 pounds. His antlers had 10 total points that were heavy and long. His rack scored 162 typical Boone and Crockett points.

A few final thoughts about this hunt. Here was a situation where a wounded buck needed plenty of time. If we had pushed him early and hard we may never have caught him. Slowly but surely, through patience and good tracking, we were able to wear the buck down and close the distance between us each time we jumped him. It was an all day hunt to be satisfied with ending about 15 minutes before last light.

Question: Dick, what kind of rifle do you hunt deer with?

Answer: A .30-06 and a 7mm Magnum.

Question: Are you into bowhunting big bucks?

Answer: I rifle and bowhunt at times, but I prefer to rifle hunt when I've got a choice. I say this because I'm into trying to kill super big bucks and an opportunity doesn't come along often. The ability to capitalize on these rare opportunities is greatly reduced with the bow because so many more conditions must be perfect. But I do really enjoy bowhunting.

Question: Dick, you probably have the best whitetail buck collection in the world. You're in constant demand as a speaker and do a lot of traveling connected with whitetail deer. What drives you? Why do you find whitetail deer so exciting?

Answer: I started collecting heads 15 years ago kind of by accident. I had to first get over the syndrome lots of people have that won't let them hang a head if they didn't kill it. I simply admired that first deer I bought for its own beauty. He was killed in British Columbia, Canada, and had 12-inch bow tines and 15 total points. It really caught my eye. Up until I bought my first head I'd always been a hard-core hunter, especially of whitetail deer. I've just always admired whitetail deer because to me they are the cleverest big game animal in the world. For a while I was living in Alaska. After four years I began to miss the whitetail so much I moved back to the lower 48. Slowly my interest in collecting, hunting, and studying the whitetail, with emphasis on big bucks, grew and grew until it became more than a hobby, almost an obsession.

The kind of deer I'm collecting now are the types of bucks a guy is not likely to see or kill in a lifetime of hunting. I'm not into collecting heads for money or prestige. I just like looking at them and showing them to other people who appreciate a superior whitetail buck. I presently have about 100 heads, and I'm constantly upgrading with better and better specimens. About 75 are nontypical and the rest are typical. I tend to prefer nontypical heads because of each one's individual uniqueness, but I do appreciate the beauty and symmetry of a big typical rack.

Whitetail deer favor the foothills areas of mountainous country for their prime habitat.

This nice whitetail buck was taken in an area of growing significance to trophy whitetail deer hunters ﹐ the eastern front of the Rocky Mountains.

Question: What are the two most important things a hunter must pay attention to in order to have a chance at collecting a trophy grade buck?

Answer: Number one above all else, a hunter has to hunt in a place where big bucks exist. You, living in the Northern Rockies, Ed, take it for granted that anywhere you hunt in the region you will find trophy bucks, and probably are right. But that is definitely not the case in most parts of the United States. Most hunters don't have that option we have in the Northern Rockies, so they need to do their homework and research the places within the individual's own state to define where the biggest bucks are found. Every state, whether it is Florida, Michigan, or Alabama will have certain areas that produce bigger bucks than others. They may or may not be Boone and Crockett caliber, but the deer will be the best that state can produce.

Number two is to have a good working knowledge of big buck behavior. This is assuming the sportsman has a handle on fundamentals like shooting, binocular work, and basic sign interpreting skills. If the basics aren't mastered, a hunter won't be ready to take a big buck when and if he is in a position to do so. The opportunity to collect a 170 Boone and Crockett point buck or better may only come once in a lifetime.

Once the basics are mastered, knowing big buck behavior will give the hunter the best chance of putting himself in the right place at the right time. Becoming a behavior expert increases the odds of putting a dream buck on the ground.

Hunting the big bucks in the high basins requires that the hunter be in good physical condition.

Question: How does a hunter learn about whitetail behavior?

Answer: Reading books helps to accelerate the learning process tremendously, but experience is, as it is with most things, the ultimate teacher. Things rarely happen by the book and that's what makes whitetail hunting so special. Just when you have all their bases covered, they pull something new and unexpected. Constant adjustment of one's thinking and actions make trophy hunting special. I'd suggest getting ahold of good reading material. Just because someone writes about deer hunting doesn't make them an expert. In other words, get knowledge from people that know.

Question: Several of the gentlemen I've interviewed for this book emphasize the point that trophy bucks are a breed apart and don't act like other whitetail deer. Gene Wensel goes so far as to almost classify them as a separate subspecies of whitetail. Would you comment on this.

Answer: There is no doubt that the truly big, older bucks are a special animal. That's not even debatable. So the big buck hunter must shift his thinking a great deal.
   I don't distinguish a 165 Boone and Crockett buck from another big, mature buck. Larger antlers don't necessarily make him smarter. In my opinion any old buck, especially if he is living in heavily hunted country, is going to be smart and just as hard to kill as a world record. Any buck that has survived four of five hunting seasons will be wise to the ways of man and will be very, very difficult to kill. They use every evasive trick in the book, but becoming almost totally a nocturnal creature is what keeps them alive. They just don't show themselves in the daylight, period.
   Something I've noticed even in areas where the older bucks have not been pressured and taught by man, is they seem to instinctively choose the only course they possibly could have to escape. Many times the buck chose, what in my mind, would have been the least likely way out of a tight spot. He chooses the alternative I least expected him to take. I've seen this phenomenon happen time and time again.

Question: Where will the next world record typical whitetail buck be taken?

Answer: I would look at areas rather than specific states. My first choice would be the Midwest, Iowa and Illinois to be exact. The bucks tend to grow real big racks that are basically clean. A very close second would be Saskatchewan, Canada.

Question: Why didn't you choose the Northern Rockies as a top candidate to produce the next world typical buck?

The dense cover of lodgepole pine and its understory have proven to be excellent habitat for whitetail deer.

Answer: Western Montana and eastern Idaho have produced very good bucks as demonstrated by the Dellwo and Petry bucks, for instance, but the bodies of both those bucks weren't as big as the Midwestern deer. In the Missouri and Yellowstone River drainages the bodies and antlers of the bucks are bigger, but the range is poorly managed, limiting the growth potential of the bucks.

The only thing that keeps western Montana from being my number one pick as the most likely spot to produce the next world record is the availability and quality of winter feed. The bucks enter the spring with emaciated bodies and all the consumed forage goes into rebuilding body tissues. Once the bodies' requirements are met, the ingested nutrients then go into antler development so the antlers lag behind the body.

The average antler base circumference of a trophy buck living in the Northern Rockies is four and three-fourths inches, while the Midwestern bucks will have a base that's bigger in circumference by one-fourth to one-half inch. The feed is the difference.

Sitting here thinking and talking, there are two areas in western Montana which are more open and offer better feed and in the future could possibly rank right up there with the Midwest. These are the Blackfoot and Bitterroot valleys.

Really, when you get down to it, the Number One typical head is a fluke of nature. The rigidity of the Boone and Crockett scoring system has made such bucks oddities and very-rare. By today's scoring standards a typical rack has to be clean, symmetrical, the tines all have to balance, and the rack must have 10 to 12 long points. What is presently scored as nontypical is more common in nature than the so called "typical" bucks.

Question: What do you perceive for the future of trophy whitetail deer hunting in the Northern Rockies?

Answer: I don't see the present state of affairs changing much except possibly increased hunting pressure because of growing numbers of hunters. The amount of heavy cover we have here should nullify the increase in hunter numbers. I think the quality of whitetail hunting will be more dependent on the length and severity of our winters, which of course varies from year to year. Montana's Fish and Game Department says hunting has no bearing on the whitetail population, but weather and winter range quality do. I honestly feel 90 percent of the bucks in the Northern Rockies are dying of old age.

This is where it all starts. In this little guy's genes is the promise of the future. Let's all help him as best we can.

In Conclusion

As you may have concluded from the preceding pages, whitetail deer have undoubtedly brought more pleasure to more people than any other wild mammal on the North American continent.

Since colonial times, the sportsman has enjoyed hunting the whitetail. It has provided sustenance for countless numbers of American families, hunters and nonhunters alike.

Deer maintain a reasonably high profile in the right situation and allow themselves to be viewed and enjoyed by large numbers of the nonhunting public. Backyard deer are a common occurrence, but so are the less apparent tracking-size animals whose lives are marked by secretiveness and isolation from people.

That is the really exciting thing about whitetail deer. They are both prolific and adaptable. They will be with us as long as the North American continent exists.

Whitetail deer hunting can be tailored to suit an individual's personal style or preference. The species can be hunted in a leisurely fashion or with a more aggressive style. Hunting techniques are limited only by the hunter's imagination. For example, some hunters are using full-body, mounted does as decoys.

The old, big bucks offer the most skilled whitetail hunter all the challenge he or she could ever imagine. Collecting trophy class bucks on a reasonably regular basis sets one apart from the everyday sportsman. And this too is possible for you if you choose to dedicate the time and effort.

Speaking personally, the time my son Scott and I have spent together hunting, photographing, and observing whitetail deer has been high quality time. Scott is only 15 years old, and I plan our hunts and show him how to read sign and how to shoot.

He's going into his fourth hunting season next year, and every year his skills improve. I used to wonder if he would become as hooked on the outdoors and hunting as I am, but not any more! Come opening day, he gets the jitters and a glint in his eye just like the old man.

The day will come, however, when dad's joints start to creak a little. I'll sit back and let Scott plan the hunt and teach old dad the latest tricks....

I wish you all easy trails-and good whitetail hunting!